paper jewellery

design & make

paper jewellery

SARAH KELLY

DISCLAIMER

Everything written in this book is to the best of my knowledge and every effort has been made to ensure accuracy and safety but neither author nor publisher can be held responsible for any resulting injury, damage or loss to either persons or property. Any further information that will assist in updating of any future editions would be gratefully received. Read through all the information in each chapter before commencing work. Follow all health and safety guidelines and where necessary obtain health and safety information from the suppliers. Health and Safety information can also be found on the Internet about certain products.

First published in Great Britain 2011
A&C Black Publishers Ltd
an imprint of Bloomsbury Publishing Plc
50 Bedford Square
London WC1B 3DP
www.acblack.com

ISBN: 9781408131442

Copyright © Sarah Kelly 2011

A CIP catalogue record for this book is available from the British Library

Publisher: Susan James
Managing editor: Davida Saunders
Series and cover design: Sutchinda Rangsi-Thompson
Page layout: Evelin Kasikov
Copy editor: Fiona Corbridge

This book is produced using paper that is made from wood grown in managed, sustainable forests. It is natural, renewable and recyclable. The logging and manufacturing processes conform to the environmental regulations of the country of origin.

Printed and bound in China

Images:
Page 1: **Oberon's Lair I Brooch**, Suzanne Beautyman. Shibuichi, knitted paper, plaster, horsehair. 2008. Photographer: Federico Cavicchioli.

Page 2: **Obverse Bracelet**, Saloukee (designed by Sarah Kelly). Paper, rivets, satin ribbon. 2010. Photographers: Jennifer Peel and Lucas Brodowicz. Model: Clare Pardoe.

Contents

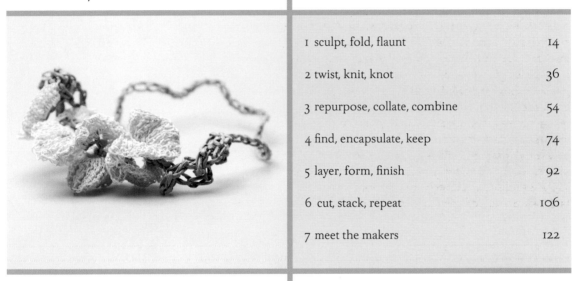
Superfrilly crocheted necklace, Sally Collins. Paper yarn. Photographer: Gemma Dewson.

For Kenneth Snowdon, for all he did to innovate, inspire and educate.

ACKNOWLEDGEMENTS

To all those who have lent me their precious time, knowledge and materials during my research and writing, I am forever grateful.

To all the makers who took the time and energy to submit images for the book: thank you. I hope you will all be inspired by my collation.

To all the galleries who have introduced me to their wonderful makers, to the Museum Bellerive in Zurich, to ATOPOS in Athens, to JIIC in Birmingham and to the Crafts Council Research Library, London: I thank you for being so informative.

To Susan James, my commissioning editor, for seeing my potential and the love for what I do; and Davida Saunders, my editor, for being so patient with my endless questions along the way.

To Sally, Jess, Clare, Paula and Soner: thank you for your wisdom, your sanity and your perfect skills.

To my wonderful photographer and treasured friend Gemma Dewson: I simply could not have done it without you!

To Joe Kay, for his undivided attention and enthusiasm whenever I needed to discuss 'the book'. I'm certain there will never be another helicopter pilot in history who is so well informed about the world of paper jewellery!

To my never questioning, always accepting Mum and Dad, my proud brothers, Graham and David, and my loyal friends: your support and understanding has been priceless.

Thank you for the faith every single one of you has had in me.

introduction

on ... paper

For designers, paper is evocative of many things, but it is also simply a familiar, basic necessity, which for centuries has provided artists throughout the world with a creative material. It has also offered people a means of recording data for various legal, religious, economic and political purposes; now digital media leads the way in these areas. Yet paper remains a tangible medium for tactile interaction in a technological world. It provides a pliable blank 'canvas' where we can translate our considered thoughts into a physical reality.

Your Job Papercut, Rob Ryan. 2010. Hand-cut from one sheet of white paper using a scalpel and then coloured with spray paint. Photographer: Liberty Wright.

Paper has been an accessible commodity for such a long time that we take it for granted. Yet the fact that it is so often overlooked seems to make it attractive to many designers. From graphic design to textiles, illustration, architecture, interior design, sculpture, product design and fashion, paper continues to prove itself as an ever-developing, incredibly versatile medium to work with. Paper provides the expressive tool that not only bridges the gap between working in two and three dimensions, but ultimately between design disciplines as a whole.

Collars for the Modern Gentleman, Michael Cepress. Paper. 2006. The collars were commissioned by ATOPOS and created for the exhibition 'RRRIPPP: Paper Fashion' at the New Benaki Museum, Athens, in 2006. Photographer: Michelle Moore. Model: Cameron McCool. Make-up: Drew Krake.

'A Costura do Invisível' Paper Garments, Jum Nakao. 2004. Jum Nakao's fashion collection, 'A costura do invisível' (Sewing the Invisible), aimed to have a playful relationship with the spectator. The intricate paper dresses were paraded on the catwalk and later torn apart during the show. Photographer: Fernando Louza. With thanks to ATOPOS, Athens.

on ... paper in jewellery

Jewellery is one of the oldest forms of body adornment and has always been held in high regard as a symbol of status and a way of augmenting beauty. Today, we continue to decorate ourselves, seeking the perfect accessories for each outfit, and paper jewellery enjoys a real prominence within the accessories market. Paper is acknowledged for its beautiful delicacy and the possibilities for it seem to have flourished in recent years, with many more designers using paper and non-precious materials than ever before.

Using paper to create jewellery 'garment transformers' is by no means a phenomenon of the 21st century. During the 1960s, innovators Wendy Ramshaw and David Watkins used paper to make modestly priced, throwaway jewellery for the mass market. The jewellery sold worldwide, from small boutiques to renowned department stores such as Harrods and Selfridges.

Something Special Paper Jewellery, David Watkins and Wendy Ramshaw. 1966–7. A selection of flat-pack paper pieces, glued or folded into the third dimension. This jewellery was very cheap and intended to be carried home flat, put together, worn once and then thrown away. The design work was shared by Wendy and David, but the finished artwork was produced by David. These ornaments caught the Zeitgeist, with flower-power motifs and day-glo colours predominating. Photographer: David Watkins.

Bracelet, Nel Linssen. Plastic-coated paper, elastic thread. 2008. Paper is clearly the material closest to Nel Linssen's heart, as she is continually driven by the need to discover logical constructions, inspired by rhythms and structures. With thanks to Galerie Ra, Amsterdam. Photographer: Bas Linssen

These flat-pack creations, designed for hand-assembly by the purchaser, fitted in perfectly with the fun fashion of the time for paper dresses, underwear, interior products and toys. Ramshaw and Watkins later went on to design a book of easy-to-wear, ready-to-make, pop-out fashion pieces. Titled *The Paper Jewelry Collection*, the book was published in 2000. Watkins later commented, 'The most important thing about the pieces is that they were improvisational in the making and they should be improvisational or informal in the wearing.'

Today, paper jewellery still raises questions about impracticality, and there continues to be a common belief that jewellery should be made from precious metals, diamonds and pearls. Yet the wearability of traditional jewellery of this kind is arguably just as limited to specific occasions. Ephemeral jewellery challenges preconceptions about durability and monetary value, yet to its makers and collectors it is embraced for its inherent values of pleasure and preciousness. Paper's true worth lies in the hands of its designer, whose accumulated skills can sculpt, knot, bind, encase, form and cut it into something that is uniquely priceless. As long as paper jewellery is treated as a wearable art form, to create a statement and to beautify, staying true to its function, it will serve its purpose and, after all, in the words of Wendy Ramshaw, 'Well, you wouldn't exactly wear a tiara on the Tube, now, would you?'

making the most of this book

Begin by flicking through the visuals in each chapter to find out which areas intrigue you. Skim-read the project that excites you most and then refer to the amazing array of international designers in the gallery section as a source of inspiration. When you're ready, have a go at the project and build on your skill set. Be sure to read the project instructions thoroughly before you begin anything practical, so you are sure about what you need and what you are aiming to accomplish.

The complexity of the projects varies. You may have used some of the techniques before, but this book will help you to build upon them and inspire you to follow new creative paths. Other techniques may be completely new to you: use the step-by-step instructions as a guide to increase your confidence. Whether you are investigating paper as a completely new medium, or whether you are looking for new techniques to complement your existing work in paper, this book will provide a starting point.

Paper Jewellery brings together the expertise of six established designers from different disciplines. This was a conscious decision, to encourage observation and innovation. Traditional skills such as bookbinding, crocheting, papier mâché, origami and silversmithing are all given a contemporary twist in the context of paper jewellery. New technologies such as laser-cutting are also explored, to illustrate the way that modern advancements can enhance jewellery-making. Use this book to spark your passion for paper and discover what an incredibly multi-faceted material it is. Above all, enjoy yourself!

tips before you begin

Collecting papers can become quite a fixation, but they must be stored correctly. Never leave paper rolled up for long periods of time, as you will have difficulty unrolling it later. Never leave paper in strong sunlight, because it will fade. Never leave paper in a damp room: the fibres will absorb the moisture and warp.

As a creative being, it is quite normal for some things to come more naturally to you than others. If a project does not go quite right the first time, be patient and do not give up. Go back through the instructions and photographs to ensure that you have not missed anything. If success still eludes you, put it to one side and return to it another day with fresh eyes. Take note of all of the useful tips and advice from designers throughout the book: you can benefit from an insider's knowledge of the world of paper and it will help you along the way.

Turn to the end of the book for recommended suppliers; before long, you will find your own suppliers, and learn which tools and methods best suit you: from here, the possibilities are endless.

The range of paper types you can choose from for your project are limitless. We recommend that you base your selection on the constructive qualities of the paper; bear in mind the requirements of your project and the results you want to achieve. For example, if your project requires the paper to be scored, folded and hold its shape, you should choose a heavyweight paper of approximately 270 gsm or above. If you need the paper to be easy to tear and translucent, choose a lightweight paper, approximately 60gsm or below. Remember to start small and as you gain confidence and knowledge you will be able to work to a larger scale. You can choose paper that is printed or plain, laminated or untreated, handmade or manufactured, bought or found: there is huge scope for exciting experimentation and successful outcomes.

1 sculpt, fold, flaunt

Folded Paper Collar, Sarah Kelly. Origami paper, organza ribbon. Photographer: Gemma Dewson. Model: Rebecca Thomas; model's hair and makeup: Megan Thomas.

Hardly a day goes by without paper passing through our hands, yet it is rarely seen as a tactile medium. Paper is unique in allowing an interaction between all manner of properties, including form, scale, function, dimension, texture and colour. It gives us the opportunity to explore practical, visual and tactile experiences of paper, which provide great stimulation for the senses. A flat sheet of paper can morph into a dimensional object that holds visual information, bridging the gap between two and three dimensions and the physical connection between the maker and their working medium.

Most people are familiar with the sculpting of paper through the Japanese art of decorative paper-folding, origami. It dates from the seventeenth century and became very popular in the mid-1900s. The word 'origami' comes from the Japanese 'oru', meaning 'to fold', and 'kami', meaning 'paper'. It is an alluring transformation of the logic of mathematics and geometry into the aesthetic of beauty. Today, the digital world also provides endless possibilities for print, pattern and information storage on the surface of paper before we sculpt it into three dimensions.

Paper lends itself perfectly to sculptural, statement-making, packaging-inspired 'pop-up' jewellery, suitable for occasional wear. This type of pop-up jewellery is now frequently seen within the capsule collections, advertising campaigns and catwalk showpieces of many well-known fashion houses. As an immediate and intuitive way of working, it allows for boundless innovation and highlights what is often a fine line between clothing, fashion and jewellery.

sculptural pleating techniques using origami papers with Sarah Kelly

WHAT YOU WILL NEED

MATERIALS
▶ Square of origami paper, any size (use 80–100 gsm printing paper as an alternative)

TOOLS
▶ Bone folder or scorer are optional

TIPS FOR FIRST-TIMERS

To begin, you need an accurately cut square of paper. The square can be any size: the larger the square, the more pleats you can create. (It is also possible to use a rectangular piece of paper: just ensure that the length is divisible by the width for the folding to work.)

Crease all folds firmly with your fingertips, or a bone folder if you prefer. The more accurately you can fold to the edges (or other specified reference points), the easier it will be as your designs gain in complexity, and the more precise the results.

In the following demonstration, a dashed line represents a valley fold (the crease will look like a valley between two hills), and a dotted and dashed line represents a mountain fold (the crease will look like a mountain ridge). These symbols are common to many origami books and diagrams.

The first six steps show you how to fold a basic grid, so you can try your hand at three completely different pleating techniques (the herringbone pleat, the diamond pleat and the water bomb pleat). When making the basic grid, fold and unfold the piece of paper for each step before moving on to the next step. Once you have grasped how to do the basic grid, further experimentation will reveal a whole host of possibilities.

BASIC GRID

1. Fold the square of paper in half to make a rectangle. Turn the paper 90° and repeat on the other side. Next, fold the paper in half diagonally to make a triangle, and then turn it 90° again and repeat, matching up the opposite corners accurately.

TIP
When the paper is unfolded, you should see that you have created two crosses through the centre of the paper.

2. Cupboard fold. Fold the edges of the paper to meet the centre line that you have just created. Turn the paper 90° and repeat.

Paper is the most appropriate material to do my work because its characteristics (thickness and firmness) make it possible to get a great compactness, solidity and steadiness without an excessive total weight.

– Elisabeth Krampe

3. **Accordion fold.** Create a pleated effect by repeatedly folding the parallel sections of paper in half to meet the lines created by the previous folds. All sides should be divided into equal parts. Once one side is folded, turn the paper 90° and repeat.

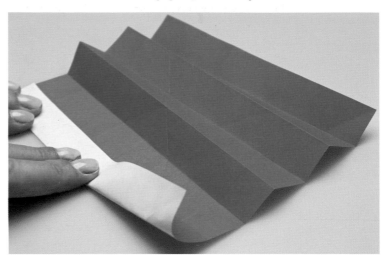

4. **Mountain and valley folds.** All origami starts with either a mountain or a valley fold. Now check that you have the correct accordion fold, with alternate mountain and valley folds. You may need to fold creases back on themselves to complete the pleat.

TIP

Getting to grips with the difference between these folds becomes very important later on, because the orientation of the folds in relation to each other will completely determine the overall shape and resistance of the paper square.

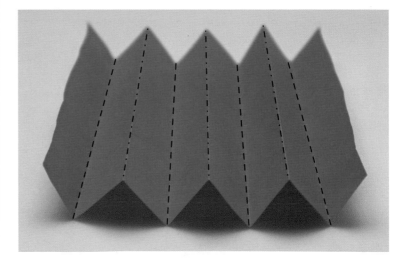

5. Create diagonal folds to divide the paper into equal parts across both diagonals. Begin by folding one of the corners inwards, lining it up at a right angle with the innermost square that you created previously. Continue to fold diagonally, using the grid of horizontal and vertical lines created by folds, until you line up the corner with the outermost square. Now repeat this with the other three corners of the paper.

6. Once you are happy that everything has been folded in equal proportions across the piece of paper, you should be left with a grid of squares with crosses through the centre of them. (Our 18 x 18 cm/7 x 7 in. paper created a grid of 8 x 8 squares.) Now make the folds 'genderless' by folding all the creases in the opposite direction. This allows the paper to sit virtually flat on the worksurface and enables you to fold more complex pleating techniques much more easily as you go forward.

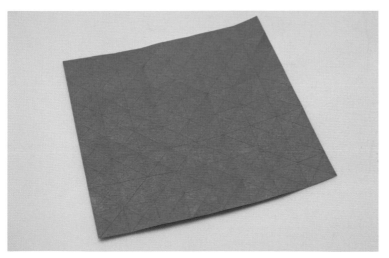

TIP

You may find that it is easier to line up the edge of the paper on the coloured surface of the paper.

TIP

Always work under good lighting conditions. A desk lamp can be used to help you to see all the creases, allowing you to make precision folds.

TIP

The centre line of the triangle should be a valley fold, and the folds to form the peak of the triangle should be mountain folds.

THE HERRINGBONE PLEAT

7. Create a basic folded grid by following steps 1–6. Refold the paper into an accordion fold (see step 4, Basic Grid). Then use your thumb and forefinger to form triangles in the first line of squares on one edge of the accordion fold.

TIP

The zigzag pattern across the paper should be a valley fold. You may find it helps to use your other hand to hold the accordion fold together as you work across the paper.

8. Carefully reverse the accordion pleat so that the valley folds are now mountain folds and the mountain folds are now valley folds. Use your thumb and forefinger to pinch ridges and pop-up pleats to help shape the first zigzag pattern.

9. As you progress, all the accordion pleats have to be repeatedly reversed, line by line. The zigzag pattern across the paper will also be alternately formed into valley and mountain folds (for example, the second line of zigzags will be folded in a mountain fold, and the third line will be folded in a valley fold, and so on).

10. Continue alternately folding the pleats and the zigzags until the entire sheet of paper is folded in the same way.

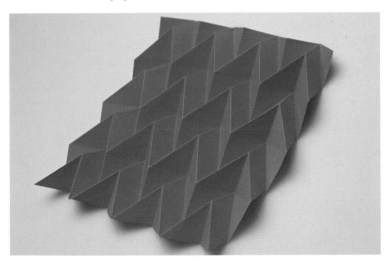

'Elephant hide paper is an excellent folding paper popular with origami and advanced folding artists. Due to the way it is sized, it can be wetted and once folded, the paper will retain its crisp edges.'

– Sarah Kelly

TIP
You should find that you can compress the finished pleat completely, and also extend and retract it in both directions.

TIP

All of these pleats are based on the art of tessellation, so you should find that the diamonds are double the size of the triangles you have just formed.

THE DIAMOND PLEAT

11. Create a basic folded grid and first line of triangles by following steps 1–6, Basic Grid, and step 7, Herringbone Pleat. Carefully reverse the accordion pleat and use your thumb and forefinger to pinch ridges and pop-up pleats to help you shape the first diamond pattern.

TIP

You should find that the diamond pleats interlock with each other, staggered alternately across the grid.

12. As you continue folding, all of the accordion pleats have to be repeatedly reversed, line by line. The folds for the diamonds in this pattern will always be a 'mountain fold', and the centre line for the diamonds will always be a valley fold.

13. Continue alternately folding the pleats and mountain-folding the diamonds until the entire sheet of paper is folded in the same way.

THE WATER BOMB PLEAT

14. Create a basic grid by following steps 1–6, Basic Grid. Refold the paper into an accordion fold (see step 4, Basic Grid), but this time, begin the pleat with a mountain fold. Start at one corner by pinching a valley-folded cross that includes four squares of the grid.

Scoring helps to reduce the stress that folding puts on your paper; it also helps to reduce the risk of cracking. For some types of heavier-weight paper, scoring is even necessary to create a clean, well-defined fold.

– Sarah Kelly

15. Review your work: each of the crosses should sit directly next to the last at the end of each mountain fold as you progress across the piece of paper.

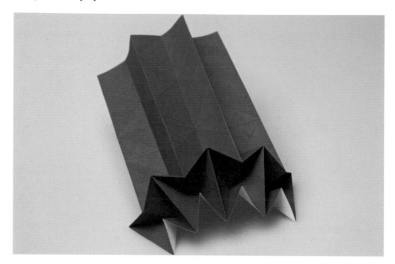

TIP

You should find that the second row of water bombs interlocks with the first row, offset to the right.

16. As you continue folding, all of the accordion pleats have to be repeatedly reversed, line by line. The next row of valley-folded crosses shifts one square along the grid. Use your thumb and forefinger to form mountain-folded ridges either side of the water bomb.

17. Continue alternately folding the pleats and valley-folding crosses until the entire sheet of paper is folded in the same way.

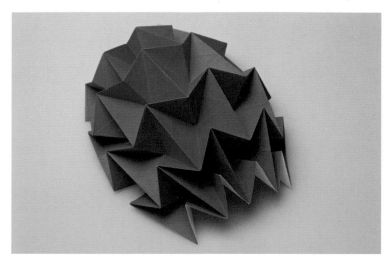

TIP

In completing the water bomb pleat, you should find that the pattern forms a hemispherical shape.

Folded Paper Collar, Sarah Kelly. Origami paper. Photographer: Gemma Dewson. Model: Rebecca Thomas; model's hair and makeup: Megan Thomas.

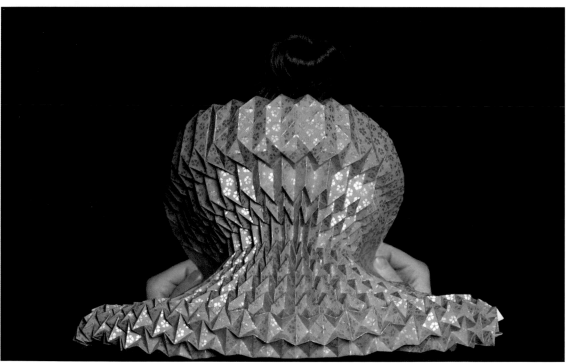

With thanks to William McCracken and Colin Smith.

gallery

1	2
	3

1 Ponk Paper Bracelet, Creative Sweatshop. Paper. 2009. Photographer: Chad Muller.

2 Repetition: Curve Neckpiece, Jae Eun Shin. Parchment paper (Pergamenata). 2010. Photographer: Jae Eun Shin.

3 Origami Neckpiece, Linsey McGregor. Murano paper, magnets, sterling silver. 2010. Photographer: Malcolm Finnie.

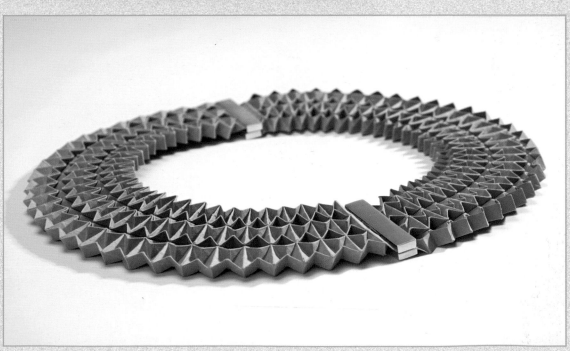

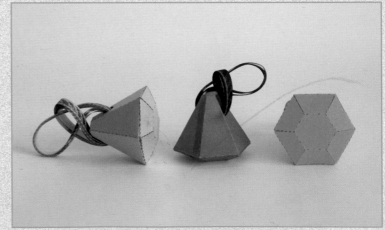

1 Euro Necklace, Tine De Ruysser. Banknotes. 2009. Photographer: Tine De Ruysser.

2 Do-It-Yourself Rings – Twine, Sarah Kate Burgess. Vellum, papers. 2006. Photographer: Sarah Kate Burgess.

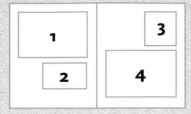

3 Obverse Collar, Saloukee (designed by Sarah Kelly). Paper, rivets, satin ribbon. 2010. Photographers: Jennifer Peel and Lucas Brodowicz. Model: Clare Pardoe.

4 All Year Rings, TT:NT (Tithi Kutchamuch and Nutre Arayavanish). Italian textured paper (200 gsm) and brown paper packaging (400 gsm). 2008. Photographer: Suratchai Chenyavanij.

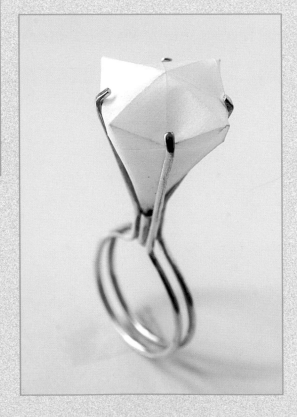

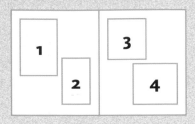

1 Sportsgirl/Alpha60, Collaboration Paper Jewels, Benja Harney. Coloured paper. 2010. Photographer: Sportsgirl Australia.

2 Royal Ring, Samantha Fung. Paper and silver. 2004. Photographer: Humberto Trejo.

3 Origami Pin, from *Paper Drops* series, Elena Salmistraro. Jackroki. 2009. Photographer: Barbara Franzò. Stylists: Erika Cigolini and Silvia Mendolia. Make-up: Ginevra Daniele.

4 Bracelet Structure I, Amina Agueznay. Paper, paint, elastic. 2007. Photographer: Mustapha Errami.

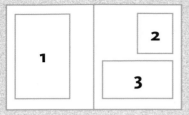

1 **Paper Necklace No. 2**, Katelyn Kronshage. Paper, thread, Plasti Dip, leather. 2010. Photographer: Justin Lackey.

2 **Necklace 2**, Fan Zhang. Corrugated paper. 2010. Photographer: Fan Zhang.

3 **Archimedean Spiral Sculpture**, Josef Baier. Cellulose. 2006. Photographer: Josef Baier.

1 Etikette Necklace, Janine Eisenhauer. Paper (chain of tags), rubber band, silver. 2004. Photographer: Friedemann Rink.

2 Necklace, Luis Acosta. Six layers of coloured paper. 2009. Photographer: Luis Acosta.

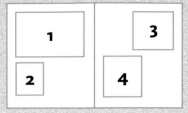

| 1 | | 3 |
| 2 | | 4 |

3 Navy Neck Scarf, Angela O'Kelly.
Hand-dyed paper yarn, plastic tubing.
2005. Photographer: Gillian Buckley. With
thanks to the Lesley Craze Gallery,
London.

4 Spiky Scarf, Zoe Keramea. Hand-
folded paper and thread. 2007.
Photographer: Zoe Keramea.

2 twist, knit, knot

Superfrilly Crocheted Necklace, Sally Collins. Paper yarn. Photographer: Gemma Dewson.

One of the most versatile forms of paper is paper yarn. It is made by cutting paper into fine strips, then folding, cording, spinning and twisting it into cords. As far back as sixteenth-century Japan, paper yarn was being used to make a woven textile called *shifu*. Samurai warriors later refined the technique to manufacture the finest threads into impressive cloths. The first industrial machines designed to produce paper yarn in Europe were developed in Germany and patented around 1900.

Today, a vast array of yarns are available in a variety of thicknesses and colours, to purchase in store and online. Many designers use paper yarn as a versatile medium to knit, weave, crochet, knot, braid, wrap, twist and tie in the very same way as other yarns are used. Surprisingly, most paper yarns can be hand-washed in warm water; they can also be dyed by hand and some yarns are even dry-cleanable. This sustainable material offers organic, lightweight, fade- and tear-resistant possibilities for paper jewellery, with huge scope for discovery. Many of the designers featured in the gallery section of this chapter feel that when working with paper yarns, it is best to trust your intuition and work in harmony with it. Though the yarns' 'hard to tame' stiffness may provide initial difficulties, experimentation and perseverance will lead to soft, supple and elegant paper creations.

'superfrilly' crochet using paper yarn with Sally Collins

WHAT YOU WILL NEED

MATERIALS
▶ Paper yarn (we've used 25 mm and 10 mm paper yarn [untwisted width])

TOOLS
▶ Crochet hooks (we've used 4.5 mm and 1.75 mm crochet hooks)
▶ Darning needle
▶ Scissors

TIPS FOR FIRST-TIMERS
The gauge of paper yarn is often indicated in number metric or 'Nm'. This is calculated by dividing the length of a yarn in metres by its weight in kilograms. You may find that your supplier will sell yarn by the length, weight, width (measured when untwisted/unfolded) and by diameter.

Choose a crochet hook that suits the gauge of the paper yarn. The easiest way to determine the right size of hook for a yarn is to see how it feels to work with. If it is too difficult to pull the yarn through the loops on the hook, you probably need to use a larger hook. Most knitting supplies shops will gladly help you with your selection.

In our demonstration we have used two yarns: a thick grey yarn and a finer white yarn. However, you can use any combination of yarns, or even the same yarn throughout: it is all about being creative and experimenting with the technique and the different effects you can achieve.

When working with paper yarn, be careful not to pull too tightly as it may snap. If it does, you have a few options:

- Unpick the work and start again with a new piece of yarn.
- Tie another piece of yarn to the broken strand and carry on crocheting, hiding the knot at the back of the work.
- Fasten off the last complete stitch and start crocheting with a new piece of yarn. You can join the two sets of stitches with a darning needle when you have finished.

CHAIN STITCH

1. Using the first yarn, tie a knot around your hook, leaving a long tail of yarn. Hold the hook in your right hand, as you would a steak knife. Wrap the yarn around the index finger of your left hand and hold the knot on the crochet hook with your left thumb and middle finger. (If you are left-handed, hold the hook in your left hand and wrap the yarn around your right index finger.) To begin creating the chain stitch, swirl the hook from left to right so a strand of the 'working' yarn lies across the hook.

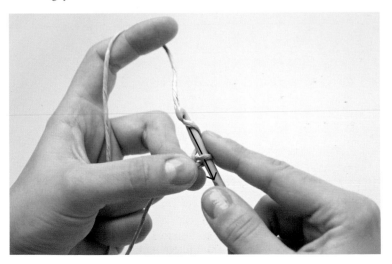

TIP
Different-sized hooks create different-sized stitches. The larger the hook, the more open a stitch will be.

2. Turn the hook downwards, so it grabs the strand, and pull it through the knot already on the hook.

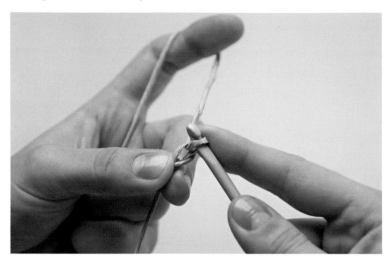

3. Keep repeating steps 1 and 2 until you have enough chain stitches for your design.

4. Cut the end of the yarn and pull the loop up and out of the last chain stitch with the hook. This is called 'fastening off' and secures the last stitch so it will not unravel (you will need to darn in this end later to complete the process).

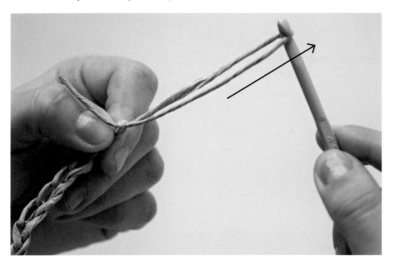

ADDING YOUR 'SUPERFRILLY' CROCHET
5. Take your other yarn and a suitable crochet hook. Tie a knot around the hook. Hold the yarn as before, this time holding the chain of stitches you have just made between your thumb and forefinger too (you will crochet into this). Insert the hook into the first large chain stitch and wrap the yarn around the hook.

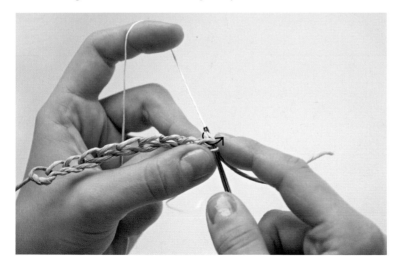

Crocheting with paper yarn can sometimes be tough on your hands when you need to maintain tension in the work by holding it stretched between your fingers. My advice is to work for short periods of time to begin with, so that your fingers don't get too sore. Once you have had a bit of practice you will get used to it and be able to work for longer.

– Sally Collins

6. Pull it back under the large stitch.

7. Pull it through the knot on the hook.

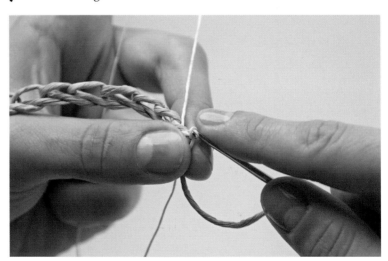

8. Make four chain stitches in the same way as for the chain (see steps 1–3, Chain Stitch).

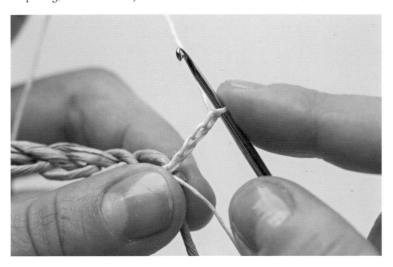

9. Wrap the yarn around the hook twice.

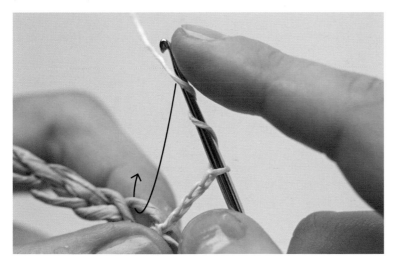

Whilst learning how to make paper, I discovered the beauty of KOZO paper by being versatile and adapting the materials and methods I was using.

– Louise Ludham

10. Insert the hook under the same first large stitch and wrap the yarn around the hook.

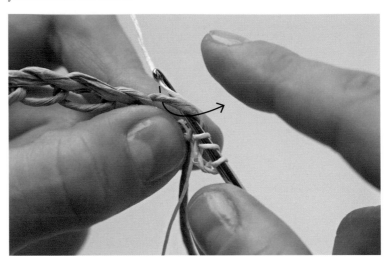

11. Pull the yarn back through (you should now have four loops on the hook). Wrap the yarn around the hook again and pull this loop through the first two loops on the hook.

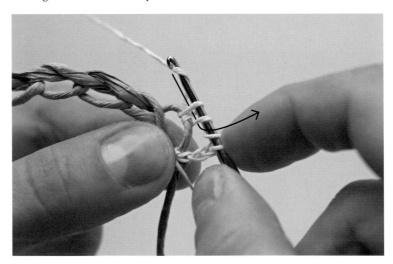

12. There are now three loops left on the hook. Wrap the yarn around the hook and pull it through two of these.

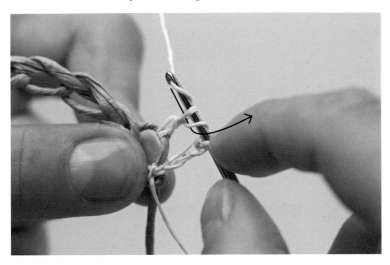

13. There are now two loops left on the hook. Wrap the yarn around the hook one last time and pull it through the remaining two loops.

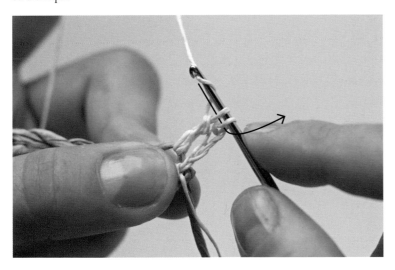

TIP

Do not worry if you make a mistake: everything can be unpicked and started again with great ease. Just simply take out the hook and gently pull on the strand of working yarn. The stitches will unravel and you can go back and start working into the piece at any point.

14. You have now finished the stitch and can start on your next stitch. At this point you should only have one loop left on your hook.

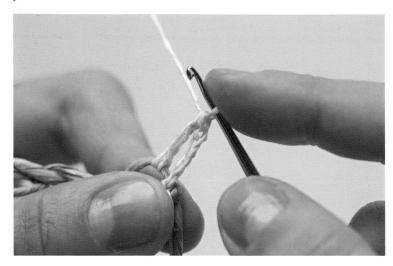

TIP

To finish the piece beautifully, use a darning needle to sew the end of the yarn into the stitches so that it is hidden.

15. Repeat steps 9–14 until you have fitted as many stitches into the first large loop as possible. When you have done this, move on to the next large loop along and crochet as before. Work through each large loop, crocheting in as many stitches as you can. Once you have finished adding all of the stitches, cut the end of the yarn and pull it through the last loop to fasten off the yarn (see step 4, Chain Stitch).

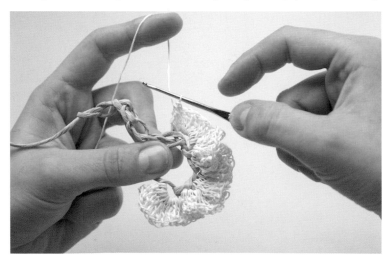

gallery

1
2

1 En Musubi Necklace, Mari Ishikawa.
Japanese kozo paper, Japanese lacquer,
silver, gold plating. 2006. Photographer:
Frank Vetter.

2 Gourds Pendants, Aimee Lee.
Naturally dyed, corded and woven hanji.
2009. Photographer: Stefan Hagen.

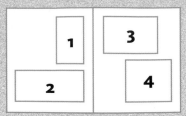

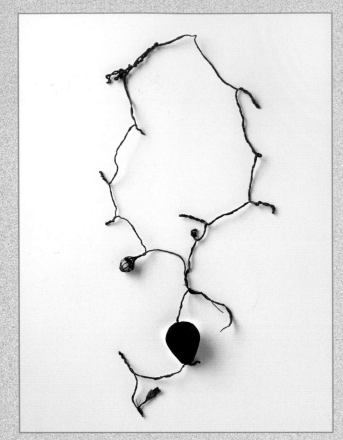

1 Grown Chain, Beatrix Mapalagama.
Paper thread, paper. 2008. Photographer:
Daniela Beranek.

2 Bride Chain, Beatrix Mapalagama.
Knitted paper thread. 2010. Photographer:
Daniela Beranek.

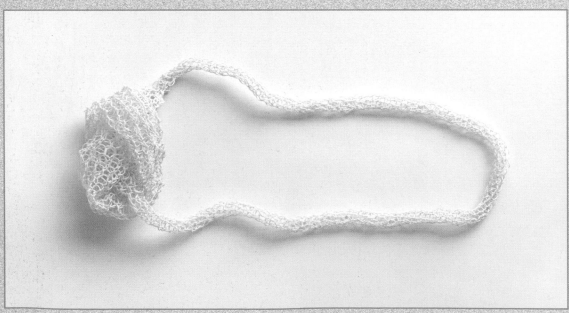

3 Blue Sea Twisted Rope Neckpiece, Fiona Wright. Evening Standard newspaper. 2009. Photographer: Full Focus.

4 Tassel Neckpiece, Jennifer Ashby. Paper yarn, sterling silver. 2009. Photographer: Jennifer Ashby.

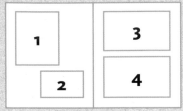

| 1 | 3 |
| 2 | 4 |

1 Paper Yarn Neckpieces Angela O'Kelly. Hand-dyed paper yarn, plastic tubing, elastic. 2002. Photographer: Trevor Hart. With thanks to the Lesley Craze Gallery, London.

2 Oberon's Lair I Brooch, Suzanne Beautyman. Shibuichi, knitted paper, plaster, horsehair. 2008. Photographer: Federico Cavicchioli.

3 Brooch, Kazumi Nagano. Woven Japanese paper, gold, silver, nylon thread, Chinese ink. 2009. Photographer: Mitsuo Shimada.

4 Due Bracelet, Linda Thalmann/ Paperphine. Industrial paper yarn. 2009. Photographer: Linda Thalmann/ Paperphine.

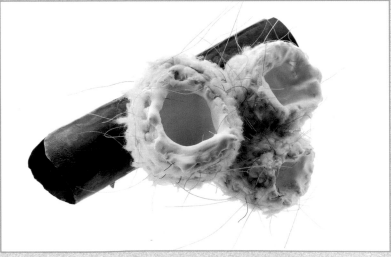

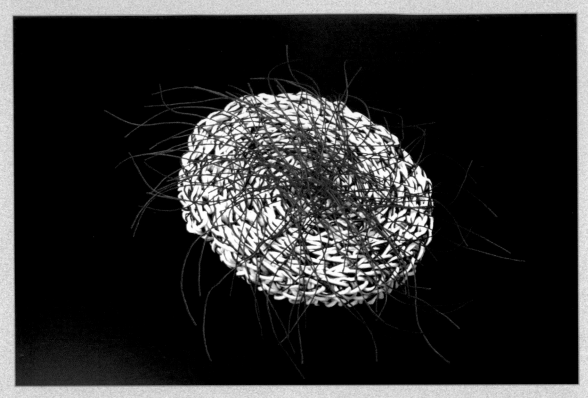

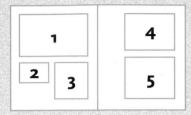

1 **Concentration Brooch**, Susan Cross. Paper, thread. 2001. Photographer: Joel Degen.

2 **Time Brooch**, Hoyeon Chung. Waxed paper, mesh, acrylic colour, rubber. 2010. Photographer: Hoyeon Chung.

3 **Kozo Neckpiece**, Louise Ludlam. Kozo paper. 2006. Photographer: Louise Ludlam.

4 **Purple Insignia Collar**, Ivano Vitali. Newspaper advertisements. 2006. Photographer: Ivano Vitali.

5 **Necklace**, Momoko Kumai. Paper, silver. 2010. Photographer: Momoko Kumai. With thanks to the Electrum Gallery, London.

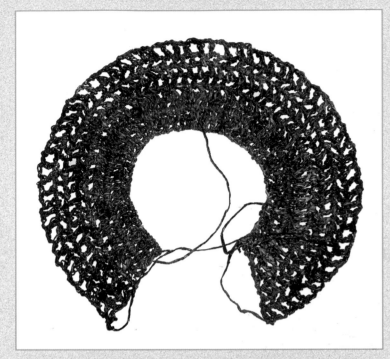

3 repurpose, collate, combine

Bound Paper Object, Paula Tew. Re-purposed paper, thread. Photographer: Gemma Dewson.

It would be disrespectful to not acknowledge, in a book about paper jewellery, what is historically one of the most seen and used forms of paper in our society – the humble book. The history of the book is rich and varied, and closely linked with the development of language, technology and culture. Books are written to be read, yet so often they are collected and displayed on bookshelves and coffee tables, becoming art objects in their own right, arguably irrespective of the content they contain.

The paper resources available to us seem to be growing, even though as a culture we have become more aware of our ecological impact, which has brought with it the challenge of recycling. With this in mind, we have become attuned to the importance of re-purposing, reconstructing and 'upcycling' paper materials. As creatives, we should champion new ways of thinking about the purposes of these papers, and pursue a wealth of techniques to make the most of this resource.

This chapter integrates the beauty of the book with the re-purposing of used paper, offering a starting point for converting what would otherwise be thrown away into wearable items of beauty. We show you a simple binding technique to give you the skills to collate, fix together and bind layers of paper decoratively and intricately within a jewellery context.

exposed-spine binding using re-purposed papers with Paula Tew

WHAT YOU WILL NEED

MATERIALS
- ▶ Card for templates
- ▶ Bookbinder's thread or other strong thread
- ▶ Paper and card of your choice for pages and soft covers

TOOLS
- ▶ Cutting mat
- ▶ Metal ruler
- ▶ Scalpel
- ▶ Bone folder or plastic ruler
- ▶ Awl or thick needle (for making precise holes)
- ▶ Scissors
- ▶ Curved needle
- ▶ Punching cradle or spine of an open telephone book

TIPS FOR FIRST-TIMERS

There are numerous ways in which it is possible to bind papers; the simple process given here will get you started. Most traditional bindings can be easily applied to recycled items, and there is the potential for developing entirely new binding methods altogether.

In bookbinding, a 'signature' refers to the folded sections of paper you bind together. We have used four pages per signature, but use your judgement as to how many you need, depending on the weight of the paper or card.

Some very basic folding is needed to create the pages that are to be bound. We will refer to both a valley fold, which is the inside of a fold, and a mountain fold, which is the outside of a fold.

This project is based on the Coptic style of binding, using a combination of papers. The signatures are pages from a book and the soft covers are made from a brown paper envelope. You may use the same papers throughout the process, or different papers for every signature. Our advice is to get creative and experiment with re-purposed papers that are precious or personal to you.

1. Cut to size and fold the desired number of signatures for your creation. If you wish, you can create a template out of card to ensure that the signatures are a consistent size. Cut and fold the soft covers (if these are to be different from the rest of the pages. In this project we have kept our signatures and soft covers the same size). You can use a bone folder to help to crease the folds.

I use only simple crafts skills such as hand-cutting and gluing. My work is neither commercial nor mass-produced, therefore the production process is inefficient. However, I do not want to use big facilities when I make my pieces, as I am being considerate of eco-friendly and energy-saving factors.

– Eiko Yoshida

TIP

You may want to make spare templates (depending on how large your binding project is), as the holes in the template are liable to get less precise the more you use it. The more accurate you can be, the more accomplished your final piece.

2. Make holes along the valley folds in the signatures. For this you will need to use a card template that is the same size as the signatures. Mark on the template where you want the holes to go: we suggest approximately 5 mm (¼ in.) from the edge and a minimum of 5 mm (¼ in.) between each hole. (In this project we have used three holes.) Open up each signature and place the template inside, then make the holes using an awl or thick needle.

3. Take a piece of thread (we found that about 75 cm/29½ in. at a time works well) and thread a needle as normal. One way to prevent the thread from escaping from the needle is to feed the needle back through the thread, then pull both pieces of thread down: this forms a loop at the bottom of the eye. Pull the loop tight and smooth it out as much as possible to avoid ripping the holes in the paper while working.

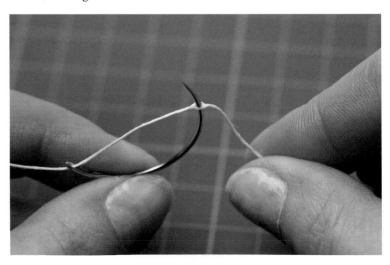

If you do need to add on thread at any point, we suggest using a 'weavers knot'. The knot should lie on the inside of the signature at the valley fold. For a weaver's knot:

Make two loops in the new thread.

Take the right-hand loop behind, up and through the left-hand loop, loosely tighten the left-hand thread to form a slip knot.

Feed your old thread through the large loop you have just created. Pull the two ends of the new thread to tighten around the old thread, which should 'snap' into place. Trim any loose ends.

Illustrations: © www.graphicalstylings.co.uk 2011

4. Take a signature and one of the soft covers (or another signature if you are not doing soft covers), and place them together. Start sewing from the inside of the first signature: take the needle out of the valley fold at hole 1, leaving approximately 5 cm (2 in.) of thread inside the first section (which will be tied off later), then insert the needle into the mountain fold at hole 2.

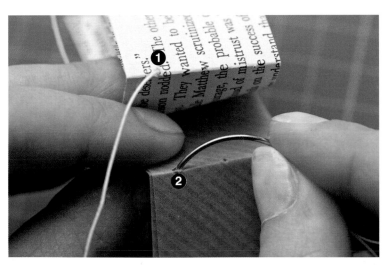

5. Bring the needle out at hole 4 and then go back in at hole 5. Exit from (the middle hole) hole 6 and insert the needle into the cover at hole 3.

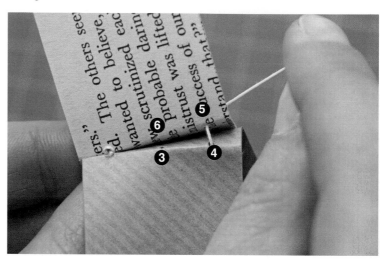

6. The thread will now be inside the cover at hole 3. Loop around the horizontal thread inside the cover. Exit at hole 3 and go back in at hole 6.

The paper I use comes from the pages of old books, some of which can be over 100 years old, and so it generally tends to be quite brittle and fragile. This is one of the qualities that draws me to paper, as it suggests history and experience, and the visual and physical effects of time passing.

– Katherine Richmond

7. Now you will be inside the first signature again. Gently tie off the thread of the loose end from earlier, trimming off the thread tail (being careful not to rip any of the holes).

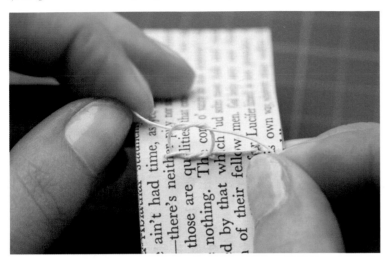

8. Take the needle back out at hole 1 and feed the needle between the first signature and the cover. Start in the gap between the hole you are at and the previous hole. Take the needle around the vertical thread (which connects the cover and the first signature) and pull the thread to form a small loop.

9. Take the needle up through the loop and pull tightly to form a knot. This is known as a kettle stitch.

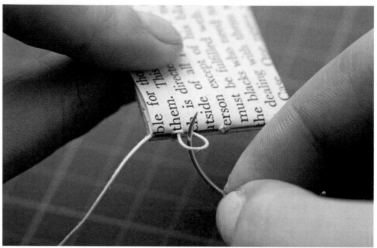

10. Take the next signature and place it on top of the last one. Insert the needle into the mountain fold at hole 7 and bring it out of the valley fold at hole 8. Again, take the thread between the first signature and the cover, starting in the gap between the hole you are at and the previous hole. For the central holes you do not need to make a knot – just loop under the vertical thread and pull tightly, forming a 'U' shape.

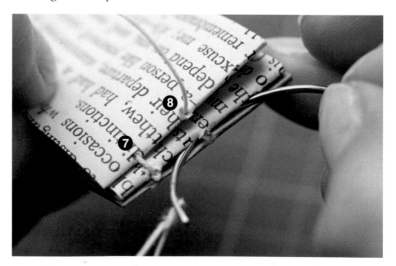

11. Insert the needle at hole 8 and come out at hole 9. Create another kettle stitch (see steps 8 and 9), but this time forming it in the opposite direction.

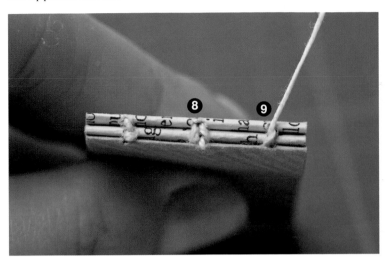

12. Repeat steps 10 and 11, but attach the next signature starting from the right. Also, you will only take the needle between the cover and the first signature when adding the second signature (as shown in step 10). As you add the third signature, you will be taking the needle between the first and second signatures; on the fourth signature, you will be taking the needle between the second and third signatures, and so on.

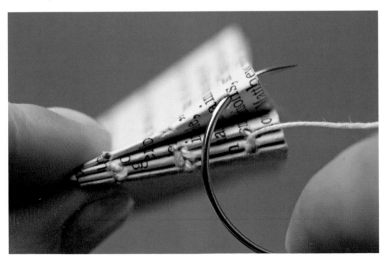

I have a deep interest in books, as literature and as objects that have been possessed and well used by numerous people. You can see the rhythm in which the books were read by the way the pages are turned or the little notes that people have made during reading.

– Jeremy May

TIP

To ensure that you are forming the stitches in the correct way, check regularly that the thread feeding through the outside holes is forming a twist pattern and the thread feeding through the middle holes is forming a chain.

13. Continue to add signatures from right to left and then left to right across the spine, until all of them have been added (except the last one if you are not using soft covers).

14. Attach the other soft cover (or final signature) in the same way as the rest of the signatures, but once the last kettle stitch has been made, insert the needle back into the hole you have just come out of. The thread will finish inside the cover or final signature.

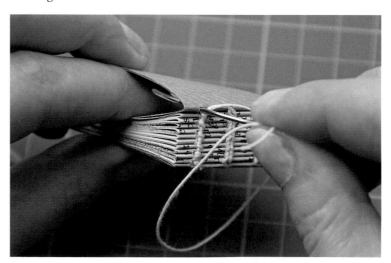

15. To finish the bound papers, simply tie the thread by knotting it around the horizontal thread twice.

TIP

For this project we have used three holes across the spine. More holes can be added, but you may want to adjust the spine length accordingly. If you choose to do this, repeat the step for central holes in step 10 and follow the other instructions as before.

Bound Paper Object, Paula Tew. Re-purposed paper, thread. Photographer: Gemma Dewson.

gallery

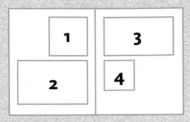

1	3
2	4

1 **'Drop My Eyes II' Brooch**, Jimin Kim. Korean paper, latex, silver. 2010. Photographer: Heo, Myung Wook. With thanks to Charon Kransen Arts, New York.

2 **Three Rings**, Clara Breen. Fine silver and found paper. 2009. Photographer: Clara Breen.

3 Sugar Flower Brooch, Eiko Yoshida. Japanese washi, book pages, twig, brass wire, brass sheet. 2010. Photographer: Lasse Johansson.

4 Jewellery Paper No. 9 Brooch, Louise Vurpas. Paper, silver. 2010. Photographer: Xavier Courraud.

1 **Westward Ho! Brooch**, Jo Pond. Silver, book cover, waxed thread, steel. 2008. **Nelson Brooch**, Jo Pond. Silver, book cover, boot button, waxed thread, steel. 2008. Photographer: Jo Pond.

2 **A Foxed Backbone Brooch**, Jo Pond. Silver, re-purposed book spine, steel. 2009. Photographer: Jo Pond.

3 **Serial no#: 045 Die Schönheit des Weiblichen Korpers, bracelet**, Jeremy May. Printed text/book; black, red and purple papers. 2009. Photographer: Eva-Chloe Vazaka.

4 **Ancient Aunt Edith's Tea Set Necklace**, Betty Pepper. Altered book, silver wire, paper, textile, thread. 2007. Photographer: Betty Pepper.

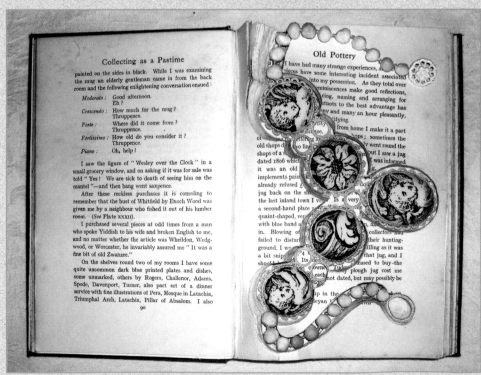

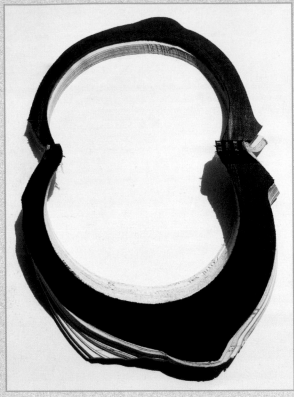

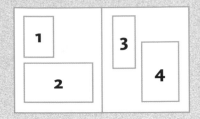

1 Orbit Neckpiece, Flora Vagi. Old book. 2009. Photographer: Flora Vagi.

2 White Sea Anemone Brooch and Grey Sea Anemone Brooch, Flora Vagi. Old book, cold enamel, gold. 2009. Photographer: Flora Vagi.

3 My Book, Chain, Beatrix Mapalagama. Book paper, thread. 2008. Photographer: Daniela Beranek.

4 Stack Sculptural Armpiece, Angela O'Kelly. Recycled postcards, elastic. 2007. Photographer: Trevor Hart. With thanks to the Lesley Craze Gallery, London.

PAPER JEWELLERY

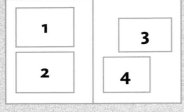

1 Today II Rings, Song Hee Park. Paper, copper, silver, brass, thread. 2008. Photographer: KC studio.

2 'To Have Is To Be' Neckpiece, Katherine Richmond. Book pages, steel pins, silver, gold plate, entomology pins. 2009. Photographer: Katherine Richmond.

3 But To Suggest Brooch, Leah Miles. Paper from damaged books, silk, glass beads, sterling silver, stainless steel. 2009. Photographer: Shannon Clegg.

4 Concer(tina) Backpiece, Kerrianne Flett. Paper, thread, brass, steel. 2009. Photographer: Jae Rae Photography.

4 find, encapsulate, keep

Encased Paper Ring and Pendant, Jessica Mason. Found paper, silver. Photographer: Gemma Dewson.

Paper is such a ubiquitous material that we often overlook and undervalue its preciousness, allowing it to be dismissed and disposed of. It is considered as 'ephemera', which is defined as 'the transitory written and printed matter not intended to be retained or preserved'. By viewing paper as ephemera, it is easy to forget its importance as a guardian of memories, and its ability to hold meanings and provide a memento to many of us throughout our lives. For example, old handwritten letters from a loved one, a dog-eared picture of a deceased relative, a favourite storybook or comic we read as a child, a travel ticket, a theatre programme, an out-of-date bank note, a map or a postcard may all invoke a sense of nostalgia and deeper emotions within us; to an outside observer, they provoke imagination and contemplation.

This chapter assumes a certain level of knowledge in silver jewellery-making techniques. It illustrates how many contemporary jewellers have sought the need to capture these memories, to preserve the past for the present and the future. By framing such treasures within jewellery to be worn, papers are taken out of their everyday context and allowed to tell their own story. In nurturing these recollections, this transient material is given longevity and its fragility is reinvented into something quite priceless.

encasing techniques using precious metals and found paper treasures with Jessica Mason

TIP

For the object to cover, use anything that is the desired size for your piece. A button makes an easy option, but you could also shape a piece of wood or plastic. Ensure that the object tapers, with the base being wider than the top – similar to the shape of a cabochon stone (this allows the correct angle for 'setting' the sample).

WHAT YOU WILL NEED

MATERIALS

▶ fine silver bezel strip (0.3 mm x 3 mm on 500g pancake reel)
▶ fine silver sheet, 0.5 mm thick (size a little larger than the base of your 'sample')
▶ silver findings
▶ extra-easy, easy and medium silver solder
▶ flux
▶ cleaning pickle (or a brass brush and pumice)
▶ object to cover
▶ decorative found paper
▶ PVA glue

TOOLS

▶ bench peg
▶ piercing saw
▶ half-round pliers
▶ flat file
▶ hide mallet
▶ bezel pusher
▶ burnisher
▶ basic soldering equipment (tweezers, soldering torch, fire brick)
▶ finishing equipment (barrel polisher/brass brush/matting pad)
▶ emery paper: coarse grade
▶ ruler
▶ marker pen
▶ strip of paper (for measuring circumference)

1. Firstly, create the paper 'sample' to encase. Do this by covering the object in layers of decorative found papers, bonding them with PVA glue. Leave the sample to dry.

In my work, the paper of each piece is rigid and therefore allows me to form the bezel around the paper by hand, with no further manipulation of the bezels.

– Mary S. McBride

· 77 ·

TIP

Leave an extra 2 mm on the length of the paper to ensure that it fits around the sample; it is easy to file off any excess.

2. Use a strip of paper to measure the circumference of the sample. Mark the measurement on the fine silver bezel strip with the permanent marker and cut it using the piercing saw on the bench peg. A piercing saw will give the cleanest cut but as an alternative, tin snips would suffice.

TIP

Do not use too much heat: the fine silver setting strip is very thin and so will get up to temperature very quickly and you have to be careful not to melt it.

The joining technique of paper to metal is key; my joins are variations on the basic techniques of riveting, screwing, tensioning, clamping and setting.

– Raimo Alberto Gabellone

3. File the edges of the bezel strip straight, and remove any burr, ensuring that there are no rough edges or sides. Bring together the two ends of the strip, using pliers if necessary. Check that the ends are accurately lined up and the join is flush. Solder the join by coating the area in flux, which has been mixed to a creamy consistency. Cut a proportionally sized piece of medium silver solder and place it directly across the join. Use a medium flame to heat the piece until the solder has run, drawing the solder through the join using the heat. Leave to clean in the pickle; once clean, file off any excess solder.

4. Shape the setting over the sample by pushing the sample through the setting using gentle pressure. Make sure that the sample fits snugly but is loose enough for you to be able to remove it. If the setting is too large, remove a section of the metal and re-solder, following the previous step. If it is too small, try stretching the setting over a bezel mandrel using a soft hide mallet: tapping it gently with the mallet down the taper of the mandrel will increase its size. Once the setting has been shaped, put the sample aside and clean off any excess solder from around the join using a flat file.

TIP

If any areas of the strip have gone out of shape, simply use half-round pliers to smooth it back into shape.

Clear resin can be a great material for encapsulating found treasures within jewellery. When working with resin, do make sure you follow the manufacturer's health and safety advice.

– Louise Miller

5. You now need to make sure the base of the setting is flat, so it can be soldered to the silver sheet (see step 6). Do this by sanding the bottom edge flat on coarse emery paper. Keep popping the sample back in the setting to check the height. The edge of the setting must be about 1 mm above the point where the side of the sample touches the silver and begins to taper in. If it is more than this, it will result in an uneven setting, so take your time.

TIP

If the setting is very uneven, use a hide mallet to tap it flat before moving on to the emery paper.

When I met my husband a few years ago, I found a lot of prints in the attic which were made by him. I fell in love with the prints and wanted to get them out into the world, so I built them into jewellery and gave them new stories to tell.

– Gudrun Meyer

6. Place the setting on the silver sheet to create the back panel; the panel piece needs to be large enough to comfortably fit the whole setting on. Solder the back panel to the setting using easy solder, making sure the solder has run around the entire join. Leave to clean in the pickle.

7. Use a piercing saw to cut neatly around the setting, then file and sand until clean and smooth.

I'm constantly looking out for old handwritten papers: the best ones are always in unexpected places, like between the pages of old books or forgotten in corners of dusty antique shops; the local flea market is often worth a visit, too.

– Clare Hillerby

8. Now the piece is starting to take shape, take your choice of findings (a ring shank, brooch, earring, cufflink findings or jump ring to link to a chain) and solder together. For this final solder join, you will need to use extra-easy solder.

TIP

Extra-easy solder has a lower melting point than medium and easy solders, so it will not require the silver to get to a hot enough temperature to risk melting previous solder joins.

9. Check that all of the solder joins are strong before using whatever methods of polishing and finishing you have available. A barrel polisher produces a shiny finish with little effort; a brass brush, wire wool or a matting pad also give a professional finish. Now gently push the sample into place by hand. Use a bezel pusher to bring over the edges of the setting, 'encasing' the sample. Do this methodically by pushing opposite sides, one at a time. Use a push 'in' and 'over' action, and once done, file and sand gently (being careful not to damage the paper sample) until clean and smooth.

TIP

If you are having difficulty fitting the sample inside the setting, use a pair of pliers to guide the metal outwards, helping to align the sample in place.

TIP

Simple curved shapes, such as ovals and circles, are easiest to use for this project. To create a square or rectangular setting, follow the same steps using pliers to sharpen the corners once the setting join has been soldered but before it is attached to the base (you may wish to further your research into bezel settings).

10. Now use a burnishing tool to smooth the edges of the setting in a flowing movement: this adds shine and a professional finish to the piece.

Encased Paper Ring and Pendant, Jessica Mason. Found paper, silver. Photographer: Gemma Dewson.

gallery

	1
2	

**1 Zueinander (To One Another)
Necklace**, Daniela Malev. Paper (drawing
on lithographic print), silver, coral, onyx.
2009. Photographer: Daniela Malev.

2 Collage Brooch, Clare Hillerby.
Oxidised silver, yellow gold, perspex,
found papers (postcard, stamps and map).
2010. Photographer: Shannon Tofts.

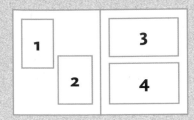

1 Book Cover Brooch with Collection Plate, Jo Pond. Silver, book cover, re-purposed enamelled collection plate, pearls, steel. 2008. Photographer: Jo Pond.

2 Forget-Me-Not Necklace, from the series 'Family Treasures', Mette Saabye. Silk, family photos. 2006. Photographer: Dorte Krogh.

3 Compass Rose Bracelet, Ela Cindoruk. Paper, elastic thread. 2007. Photographer: Ela Cindoruk.

4 Oval Claw-Set Image Necklace, Antonia Chiappe. Silver, photograph on card, polycarbonate sheet. 2010. Photographer: Antonia Chiappe.

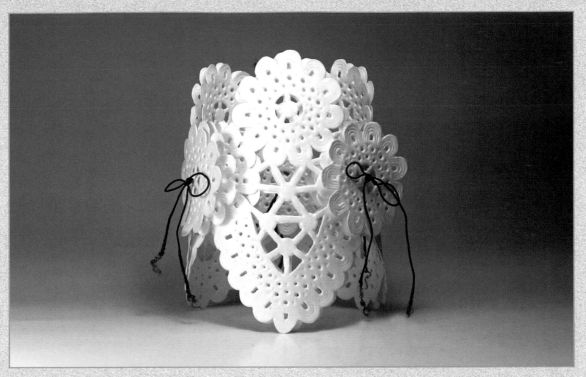

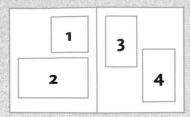

1 **Pendant la Nuit – 2:37 a.m.**, Mary S. McBride. Newspaper, antique tissue paper, paint, sterling silver. 2010. Photographer: Kevin Duffy.

2 **Love Token, Engagement Rings #1–5**, Anika Smulovitz. Ferrero Rocher chocolate wrappers, Russell Stover chocolate boxes, Hershey's Pot of Gold chocolate boxes. 2002. Photographer: Anika Smulovitz.

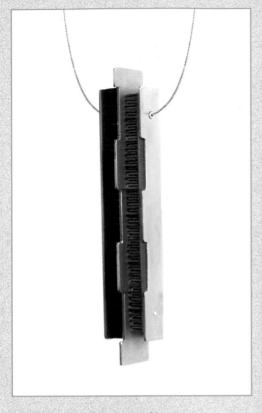

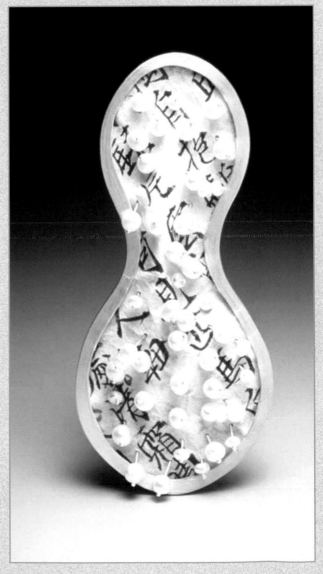

3 Paper Construction 0410 Necklace, Raimo Alberto Gabellone. Cotton rag paper, pigment ink, titanium, silver, stainless steel. 2010. Photographer: Raimo Alberto Gabellone.

4 Beauty of Nature Brooch, Kiwon Wang. Silver, pearl, antique Korean poetry book. 2008. Photographer: James Beards.

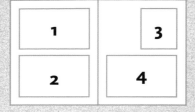

| 1 | | 3 |
| 2 | | 4 |

1 Cherished Memory, Brooch, Leila Arzaghi. Gold-plated silver, tea bag. 2009. Photographer: Lida Arzaghi.

2 Unnatural Camouflage Brooches, Märta Mattsson. Wallpaper, painted cicada, resin, walnut wood, silver. 2010. Photographer: Amanda Mansell.

3 Ring 1, Made in Paper, Anna Orska. Brass, coloured paper. 2009. Photographer: Krzysztof Dąbrowski.

4 Constance Pendant, Gudrun Meyer. Sweet wrapper, silver, topaz crystal chain. 2010. Photographer: Marcus Kiel.

creating moulded forms using tea bag paper with Clare Goddard

I chose paper because of its humility and friendliness. I don't have to fight with paper: I can just touch it and try to translate the old forest, with its sounds and colours, and my joy at playing in it.

– Ana Hagopian

WHAT YOU WILL NEED

MATERIALS

▶ lightweight paper (tissue paper or tea bag paper)
▶ solution of washing-up liquid and water in equal parts
▶ mixture of equal parts glue and water (wood glue or PVA glue)
▶ cotton thread
▶ colourants or dyes (optional)
▶ thread and materials for surface decoration (optional)

TOOLS

▶ a utensil or solid, waterproof object to use as a mould
▶ paintbrush
▶ scissors
▶ needle

1. Select a utensil or a solid, waterproof object to make a mould from (we have used a spoon). Lightly coat the mould with the washing-up liquid solution, using a paintbrush. (This will help you to release the paper form from the mould on completion.)

2. Tear up the paper into tiny strips and dip or coat them with the glue mixture. Cover the entire surface of the mould with an even layer of paper, ensuring that you bend the paper around the mould.

The paper I use for my jewellery is mainly from South Korea and is called HANJI*; it is made of mulberry tree fibre. I press the paper with water by hand, creating a beautiful wrinkled texture. This technique is called* JOOMCHI *and is traditionally used in Korea to make purses, raincoats and furniture.*

– Myung Urso

TIP

As you layer the paper, criss-cross it in all directions: this makes the form as strong as possible.

I use ready-made paper, newspaper and doilies, which are all very thin so I paste together several layers and cut them to my liking. I then make them stronger by applying paint and varnish in order to make them water-resistant.

– Ela Cindoruk

TIP

Bear in mind how you want to finish and use your design, as this will determine the number of layers you need to apply. Add more if the form needs to be particularly strong; add fewer if you would like it to be more delicate or plan to stitch into it.

I found that Japanese mulberry paper worked best at absorbing epoxy resin. I was able to convey the delicacy of the object, and still have strength in the structure.

– Sharlaine Anapu

My choice of materials best translates my fascination with translucency, fragility and the ephemeral beauty that exists in nature and presents the wearer/viewer with tangible expressions of this almost intangible beauty.

– Sabrina Meyns

3. Build up the layers gradually, until you have a minimum of ten layers of paper. Leave each layer to dry completely before adding the next layer. The picture shows the spoon when two, five and ten layers of paper have been applied.

4. When you have added all the required layers and the paper shape is completely dry, carefully lift it from its mould. With a sharp pair of scissors, trim away the excess paper to give a clean, finished edge.

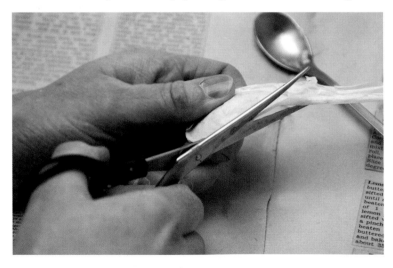

5. If there are delicate areas in your design, it is a good idea to strengthen the form by hand-stitching it. Gently bend the paper edge downwards and stitch the paper from one edge to the other in a criss-cross formation. You may also wish to use a straight stitch to create a hem around the entire shape.

TIP

Stitching not only gives strength to a form and helps it to retain its shape, but it can also add beautiful detail.

I find that stitched paper is actually quite strong and experimentation is crucial; try all the materials and methods you can.

– Katelyn Kronsage

6. Now you are free to get creative. If you wish to hang or wear the piece, puncture a hole and feed thread through it. If you wish to add surface decoration, colour or treatments, these can be applied at your leisure.

TIP

Try varnish and lacquer, writing and printing, or painting and drawing. Collage wallpapers and magazines, or colour papers with food colourings and natural dyes.

gallery

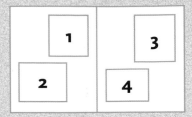

| 1 | 3 |
| 2 | 4 |

1 Fat and Tall Rings, Annette Kortenhaus. Papier mâché, coloured paper. 2001. Photographer: Annette Kortenhaus.

2 Reside 1 Brooch, Mary Hallam Pearse. Paper, sterling silver, faux aquamarine. 2005. Photographer: Mary Hallam Pearse.

3 Untitled Necklace, Attai Chen. Paper, acrylic paint, coal, wood glue, linen. 2010. Photographer: Mirei Takeuchi.

4 Untitled Brooch, Sabrina Meyns. Hand-made paper, seeds, fine silver, stainless steel. 2009. Photographer: Aspect Photography.

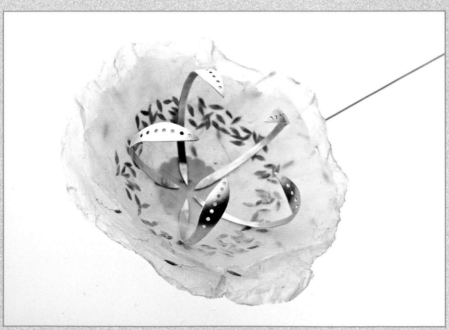

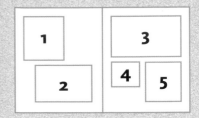

1 The Springtime of Life Necklace, Ji Eun Lee. Sterling silver, paper, thread, wire. 2008. Photographer: SCAD.

2 'Dreams About Dreams' Bracelet Mi-Mi Moscow. Paper, melchior. 2007. Photographer: Mi-Mi Moscow.

3 'Egg' Rings, Sharlaine Anapu. Japanese paper with epoxy resin, blackened silver, gold rivet, gold leaf. 2009. Photographer: Sharlaine Anapu.

4 Vicenza Ring, Barbara Uderzo. Yellow Pages paper, silver, crystal, 2006. Photographer: Barbara Uderzo.

5 Abacá Ring 1, Melissa Walter. Hand-made abacá paper, sterling silver, resin. 2010. Photographer: Melissa Walter.

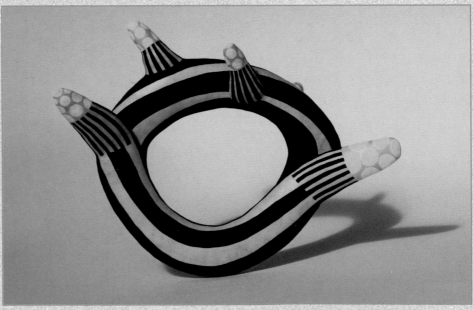

1 Amaryllis Necklace, Ana Hagopian. Paper. 2009. Photographer: Fabián Vázquez.

2 Groucho Necklace, Biba Schutz. Sterling silver, hand-made flax paper, adhesive. 2009. Photographer: Ron Boszko.

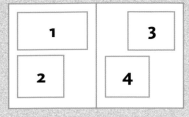

3 **Untitled Necklace**, Fabrizio Tridenti. Paper, epoxy resin, aluminium, iron, electric wire. 2009. Photographer: Fabrizio Tridenti.

4 **Daisy Necklace** from the series *Grandfather's Stamp Collection*, Mette Saabye. Stamps, papier mâché, silk. 2006. Photographer: Dorte Krogh.

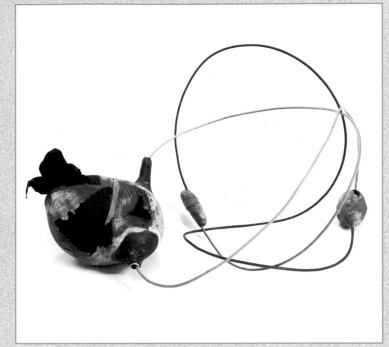

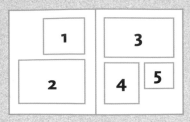

1 | 3
2 | 4 | 5

1 **'Shed' Necklace**, Midori Saito. Sterling silver, gold, paper, resin, thread. 2009. Photographer: Midori Saito.

2 **Ordinary Beauty Ring**, Inni Pärnänen. Burnt and dyed household paper, candle wax, iron and cotton thread. 2009. Photographer: Inni Pärnänen.

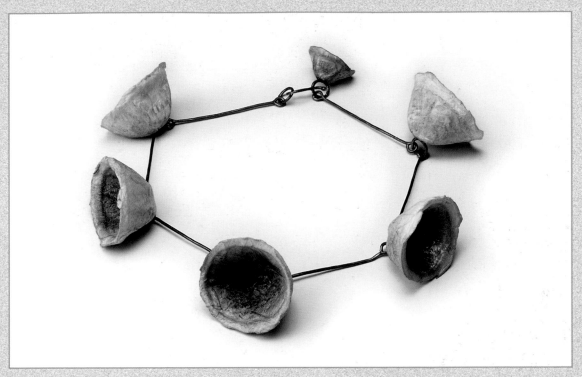

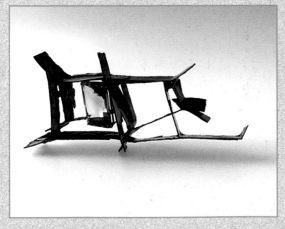

3 Song of Songs Necklace, Myung Urso. Korean mulberry paper, oriental ink, sterling silver, lacquer. 2009. Photographer: Tim J. Fuss.

4 Shining Cocoon Necklace, Luise Herb. Hand-made paper, gold leaf, cord. 2008–09. Photographer: Luise Herb.

5 Brooch, Lilli Veers. Silver, amethyst, paper, resin. 2006. Photographer: Lilli Veers.

6 cut, stack, repeat

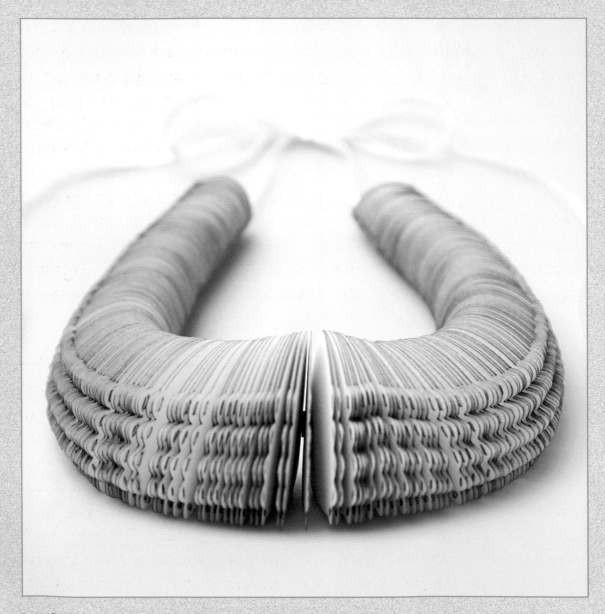

Laser-Cut Necklace, Sarah Kelly. Paper, ribbon. Photographer: Gemma Dewson.

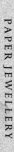

There is nothing quite so universally accessible as a sheet of flat A4 paper. Yet this can be transformed into something quite extraordinary with a crisp cut, a sleek slice or tentative tear. Paper-cutting is an ancient craft, popular throughout the world. It requires only simple tools and a great deal of time and patience. In some cultures, only scissors are used; in others, sharp blades; and in others, particularly in Japan, paper is folded before cutting, a craft known as *kirigami*.

This engineering of paper in its two-dimensional form frequently requires great quantities of material to create any form of mass, and advancements in technology have helped with this task. With the invention of die-cutting and stamping machinery and other innovations, it has become possible to perform great quantities of precision cuts in all manner of materials, with paper products benefiting from the advancements greatly.

Paper-cutting has moved on from a craft base to being technology-led. For many jewellery designers, the use of repetition is often central to a design and can also be visually appealing. Stacked layers may be employed to achieve mass and fulfil the function of movement within a piece of wearable jewellery. Lasers provide an ever-developing method for the precision cutting of paper. The direction, speed and intensity of the laser beam are controlled by digital files read by a computer. More and more designers in industry rely on laser-cutting for precision and the increased productivity it brings. This chapter will show you how to produce a digital design file to send for laser-cutting; use your creativity to take this knowledge further and tap into the endless possibilities that laser-cutting offers to jewellery designers.

laser-cutting multiples using manufactured papers with Sarah Kelly and Soner Ozenc

WHAT YOU WILL NEED

MATERIALS
▶ paper of your choice (we've used a 270 gsm heavyweight paper)

TOOLS
▶ computer
▶ Inkscape, Adobe Illustrator or CorelDraw software

TIPS FOR FIRST-TIMERS

You need to provide the laser-cutting supplier with a vector image. The most frequently used software programs to create this are Adobe Illustrator, CorelDraw and Inkscape. For purposes of accessibility, we have used Inkscape (version 0.48) in this project. This free, open-source software is compatible with SVG (Scalable Vector Graphics) and EPS (Encapsulated PostScript) file formats.

This project assumes a basic knowledge of design packages. If you are a complete beginner, download Inkscape from inkscape.org and try one of its many tutorials to get to grips with the basic tools and navigation. Alternatively, your local college may provide a suitable course. You can also find a lot of information online.

Each laser-cutting supplier will have particular specifications, so it is important to understand these and raise any queries before you send a file – clear communication throughout the process is important. The following project, which gives you some guidelines, used the services of razorlab.co.uk. Their system enables you to upload a design, choose the material, get instant pricing, pay online and get it delivered to your door.

I learned that Tyvek quickly dulls steel blades, but discovered an alternative in thermal-kiss cutting, which uses warm magnesium plates instead of sharp blades to melt out the edges of the specific shapes from the Tyvek sheet.

– Carol-lynn Swol

1. Document size set-up The size of your document and the layout of the artwork (i.e. the graphic or drawing) on your material will be specified by the supplier according to the dimensions of their laser bed. Use `File > Document Properties`, then select the 'Page' tab and enter the custom height and width, ensuring that the correct unit of measurement is selected. (N.B. Our supplier provided a downloadable design template that allows you to design in a specified area, with the document size locked.)

When cutting paper by hand, use a scalpel or craft knife with a 30° angled blade.

– Li-Chu Wu

2. Drawing a design and importing images The core of the design will be the shapes that you want to have cut out. Inkscape, along with other vector design programs, provides a toolbar. This helps you to generate several versatile shapes which can easily be moved, scaled and rotated. The freehand and Bézier tools, with their inbuilt nodes, allow the drawing of arbitrary (unassigned or undetermined) and regular paths. The more practised you become, the more advanced your designs can be.

TIP

It is also possible to use hand-drawn sketches. These can be scanned and imported into the artwork. The scanned images can then be converted into vector format by using the trace bitmap tool.

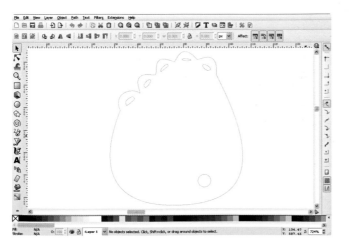

Vellum is mammal skin prepared for writing or printing on. I use it for its paper-like and fragile appearance.

– Märta Mattsson

3. **Line thickness set-up** The drawing line needs to be a certain thickness (as specified by the supplier) in order for it to be interpreted as a laser-cutting line. Select your design. Use `Object > Fill and Stroke`, then set the 'Stroke Style' tab, entering a custom stroke width and ensuring that the correct unit of measurement is selected. (N.B. In our design, the cutting lines are no closer together than 0.5 mm. Our supplier's laser burns away around approximately 0.2 mm each time it makes a cut, so any areas where the cutting lines are too close together could be burned away. Ensure that you design to suit your supplier's specifications.)

TIP

It is also possible for a laser to engrave, or raster, the surface of a material. This requires a different colour for the cutting line. If this is something you would like to explore, ask the supplier for the set-up presets.

4. **Line colour set-up** The drawing line needs to be a certain colour (as specified by your supplier) in order for it to be interpreted as laser-cutting line. Select your design. Use `Object > Fill and Stroke`, then set the 'Stroke Paint' tab and enter the custom RGBA values.

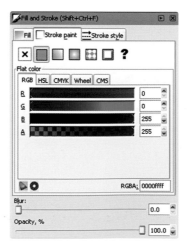

5. **Repeating your design** The beauty of laser-cutting is that you can replicate the same design over and over again and get a perfect repeat, which is advantageous when making stackable jewellery. It is also ideal when using the same design, but at a different scale, for varying types of jewellery – for example a necklace and earring set. It is easy to duplicate, scale up or scale down a design and distribute it across the document. Select your design. Use `Edit > Copy`, `Edit > Paste`, then move the duplicate as required.

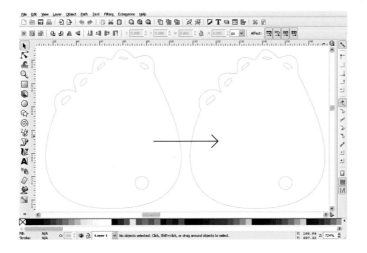

TIP

Your supplier may have a preference for your artwork layout. They may even have specialist nesting software to help distribute the design in the most efficient manner. Ensure that you clarify this before laying out your designs in the document.

6. **Optimising your design** One of the most common mistakes that suppliers find when they receive a file is the presence of double cutting lines. It is important to delete double shapes to prevent the laser from cutting the material twice. You should be able to see doubles quite plainly as being a darker colour than other cutting lines. Select your design. Use `Edit > Delete`.

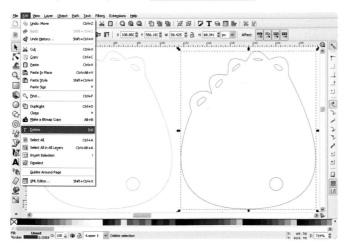

TIP

To optimise your design and reduce production costs you can make objects share cutting lines. If you have two or more objects with parallel lines, you can lay them side by side and remove one of the now-overlapping lines. This means that you are effectively cutting out two pieces at once.

TIP

A laser cuts at different speeds, depending on the thickness of the material. The burning on the edge of the paper (or heat-affected zone, HAZ) is also more apparent on thick materials than thinner ones. Your supplier may be able to offer a solution to minimise the burning if this is important for your outcome.

7. **Trialling a design** To save time and money, we suggest that you check the design thoroughly before sending it to the supplier. Print out the design on paper as an instant first prototype. Before you print, adjust the width of the stroke lines to simulate the actual thickness that the laser will burn away (kerf width) – our supplier's kerf width is 0.5 mm. This will help you to identify any areas that are too finely detailed and give you a general feel for the final result.

TIP

It is unlikely that you will create a perfect piece of jewellery on your first attempt. It usually takes a prototype or two to get a design right. With this in mind, we suggest starting small before committing to a bigger project.

8. **Save and send the file** When you are confident that the design is correct, save the file and send it. The supplier will specify the file format and the method of delivery. Use `File > Save As`, input your chosen file name, then select the format from the 'Save as Type' drop-down menu. Click Save.

With thanks to research fellow, Dr Ann-Marie Carey of BIAD Research Department.

gallery

	1
2	

1 In the Twilight Brooch, Kaoru Nakano.
Japanese paper, silver. 2008.
Photographer: Kaoru Nakano.

2 Monologue Necklace, Myung Urso.
Korean mulberry paper, oriental ink,
sterling silver, lacquer. 2010.
Photographer: Tim J. Fuss.

1	3
2	4

1 Compass Necklace, Francesca Vitali. Re-purposed paper, sterling silver, nylon-coated steel cable, magnet. 2010. Photographer: Francesca Vitali.

2 'Faltungen' Necklace, Elisabeth Krampe. Elephant hide black paper, red oil paint. 2009. Photographer: Brigitte Sauer.

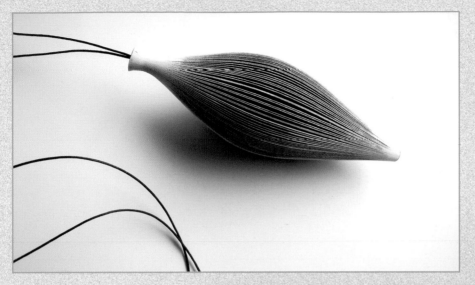

3 Simultaneity Pendant, Michihiro Sato. Paper (magazine), silver, brass, string. 2007. Photographer: Michihiro Sato.

4 No Title Necklace, Lydia Hirte. Thin cardboard, painted and glazed; natural silk thread. 2009. Photographer: Jürgen Kossatz, Dresden.

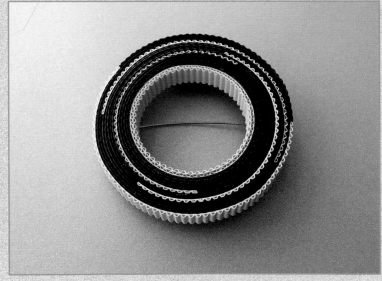

1 **Corrugated Cardboard Brooch Combinations**, Ritsuko Ogura. Corrugated cardboard, silver, acrylic colour. 2007. Photographer: Hitoshi Nishiyama. With thanks to the Alternatives Gallery, Rome.

2 **Brooch**, Anne Finlay. Corrugated cardboard. 2010. Photographer: Anne Finlay. With thanks to the Lesley Craze Gallery, London.

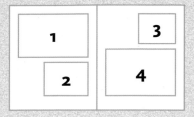

3 **Solitary Bracelet**, Saloukee (designed by Sarah Kelly). Paper, rivets, satin ribbon. 2010. Photographer: Gemma Dewson.

4 **Untitled Brooch**, Li-Chu Wu. Paper, silver. 2010. Photographer: Hsiao-Chiao Juan.

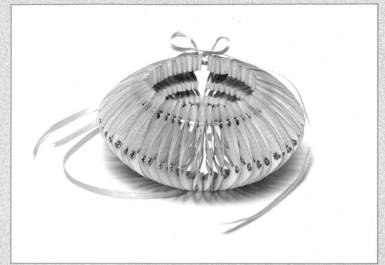

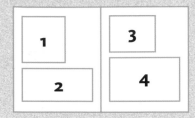

1	**3**
2	**4**

1 Food Label Chicken Pin, Melanie Codarin. Recycled card, steel pin. 2010. Photographer: Melanie Codarin.

2 Sisyphus II Necklace, Anne Achenbach. Package of confetti (100g paper), elastic. 2009. Photographer: Anne Achenbach.

PAPER JEWELLERY

3 **Blue Shell Necklace**, Naoko Yoshizawa. Japanese paper, oxidised silver. 2010. Photographer: Naoko Yoshizawa. With thanks to the Lesley Craze Gallery, London.

4 **Hoodoo Channel Brooch**, Carol-lynn Swol. Tyvek, sterling silver, stainless-steel wire. 2006. Photographer: Carol-lynn Swol.

	1		4
2		3	5

1 White Sculptural Armpiece, Angela O'Kelly. Japanese paper, fine silver, wire. 2005. Photographer: Trevor Hart. With thanks to the Lesley Craze Gallery, London.

2 Bevelled Slate Bracelet, Susanne Holzinger. Glued layered paper, carved. 2008. Photographer: Susanne Holzinger.

3 Tinted Paper Ring, Nan Nan Liu. Paper, silver. 2007. Photographer: Nan Nan Liu.

4 Wing Necklace, Märta Mattsson. Vellum made from goat, butterflies, nylon thread. 2010. Photographer: Dominic Tschudin.

5 Jewellery Paper No. 1 Necklace, Louise Vurpas. Paper, silver. 2010. Photographer: Xavier Courraud.

meet the makers

Sally Collins

For further information, please visit
www.sallycollins.co.uk or contact Sally directly at:
sallycollins@live.co.uk

Photographer: Melody Cole.

Where did you do your degree or training?
I gained an MA with distinction in Silversmithing, Jewellery and Related Products, at the School of Jewellery, Birmingham City University, in 2008.

What is your current job and/or practice?
I am a designer-maker and a lecturer for BA (Hons) Silversmithing and Jewellery at the School of Jewellery, Birmingham City University.

What is your specialism?
Combining traditional metal-smithing skills with traditional textile techniques.

What is your top tip for working with paper?
Once you feel confident with the crochet stitches, just be creative and playful with the technique. Experiment with it and make it your own, then you'll have a truly unique and fabulous creation!

Is there an ambition that you have yet to fulfil?
I am yet to create the most 'Superfrilly' and exuberant neckpiece of my collection; I want to make one real pièce de résistance!

Clare Goddard

For further information, please visit
www.claregoddard.com or contact Clare directly at
studio@claregoddard.com

Photographer: Sven Wiederholt.

Where did you do your degree or training?
I studied for an MA in Textiles at the Royal
College of Art, 1991.

What is your current job and/or practice?
I am a designer-maker.

What is your specialism?
Collage.

What is your top tip for working with paper?
Explore and experiment with the qualities of
different papers.

Is there an ambition that you have yet to fulfil?
I want to do larger-scale work and more
conceptual pieces.

Sarah Kelly

For further information, please visit
www.saloukee.com or contact Sarah directly at
info@saloukee.com

Photographer: Gemma Dewson.

Where did you do your degree or training?
I gained a BA in Three-Dimensional Design:
Jewellery and Silversmithing from Loughborough
University in 2005.

What is your current job and/or practice?
I am a 3D designer, part-time lecturer, workshop
leader and author.

What is your specialism?
Laser-cutting and 3D paper manipulation.

What is your top tip for working with paper?
Be patient, persevere, always enjoy what you
are doing, trust your instinct and let what feels
right drive you. Stay true to your vision, however
eccentric it may be!

Is there an ambition that you have yet to fulfil?
Working on larger scale for the fashion industry,
and doing collaborative work with furniture,
interior and product designers.

Jessica Mason

For further information please visit
www.jessicaelizabeth.co.uk or contact
Jessica directly at *info@jessicaelizabeth.co.uk*.

Photographer: Marcel Walker.

Where did you do your degree or training?
I gained a BA in Three-Dimensional Design:
Jewellery and Silversmithing, at Loughborough
University in 2005.

What is your current job and/or practice?
I am a jeweller, workshop leader and teacher.

What is your specialism?
Precious metal jewellery and education.

What is your top tip for working with paper?
When making paper jewellery you may have
to be prepared to (at the very least) justify your
choice of material, or in the extreme, prepare for
a challenging debate! Enjoy breaking the mould
and ruffle a few feathers along the way!

Is there an ambition that you have yet to fulfil?
I am moving towards further experimentation
with mixed media, but I will never abandon
my skills as a silversmith, which epitomises
perseverance and craftsmanship. I hope to
combine mixed media and precious metals in a
way that encapsulates both creativity and quality.

Soner Ozenc

For further information,
please visit *www.sonerozenc.com* or contact Soner
directly at *soner.ozenc@razorlab.co.uk*

Photographer: Kate Wood.

Where did you do your degree or training?
I have an MA in Industrial Design, from Central
St Martins College, 2005.

What is your current job and/or practice?
I am a product designer and laser cutting
consultant.

What is your specialism?
Product design and laser-cutting technology.

What is your top tip for working with paper?
With the correct power and speed settings,
paper is an excellent material to laser-cut and also
engrave. Experimentation is the key; it will take
a number of prototypes to excel in this area.

Is there an ambition that you have yet to fulfil?
To become a pioneer in the digital manufacturing
field in the UK, and combine not only laser-
cutting but also 3D printing and CNC.

Paula Tew

For further information please visit
www.paulatew.co.uk

Photographer: Gemma Dewson.

Where did you do your degree or training?
I studied at Birmingham City University for an
MA in Textiles, Fashion and Surface Design;
I graduated in 2005.

What is your current job and/or practice?
Visual artist and educational practitioner.

What is your specialism?
Print and repeat pattern.

What is your top tip for working with paper?
Although paper can be fragile, it can be very
forgiving: folds can be refolded and holes can
be filled in if you make a mistake or change
your mind.

Is there an ambition that you have yet to fulfil?
To revisit Japan, where I lived for three years, and
to get more involved with exhibiting my work.

paper list

The following is not a definitive list of paper types but instead a guide that can be used as a starting point for experimentation and to inspire your creativity.

Abacá Paper Also known as Manila Hemp, this is a paper made from a species of banana, native to the Philippines. It is mostly processed into specialist paper; it is commonly used to produce tea bags and currency.

Acid free paper Paper free from acid-producing chemicals, which is therefore more durable and less prone to yellowing.

Archival paper This term is loosely used to describe paper with long-lasting qualities, that are acid and lignin free, and usually have good colour retention. Its name comes from the fact it is often used by archivists and librarians for keeping records.

Cartridge paper High-quality, textured and heavy-weight paper, this is typically used for illustration and watercolour painting, for its strong and resistant surface.

Coated paper As the name suggests, the surface of this paper is coated by a compound such as china clay, latex or starch, which gives a smooth, gloss, matt or satin finish. It is sometimes also called art or gloss paper.

Cotton paper Also known as rag paper, this paper is made from cotton fibres. It has superior strength and durability to paper made with wood pulp and is often used to make modern bank notes.

Elephant hide paper This durable paper is available in varying weights and colours, and is best known for its use in wet folded origami and as covers in bookbinding.

Esparto paper This variety of grass is used as a fibre in paper making, particularly in high quality book manufacture.

Flax paper Plant fibre that can be used in paper making; also known as 'linseed'.

India paper Traditionally used for Bibles and dictionaries, this high quality, opaque rag or hemp paper is very thin, but strong.

Inkjet paper Designed for use in inkjet printers, this fine paper is classified by its weight (in gsm), its brightness and its smoothness. It is a useful medium for printing because it counteracts the spread of ink. For low quality printing, printing paper will suffice (see printing paper).

Jacroki An Italian, patented material made of natural and recycled paper fibres.

Joomchi paper Textured paper that is made using a traditional Korean technique involving layering and agitating fibres by hand.

Kozo paper Fibre from mulberry plants, the most important plant in Japanese paper-making, is used to make a type of paper often called 'Kozu'.

Kraft paper Machine-made, this paper is created from wood pulp, and its name derives from the German word for 'strong'. Its appearance can be natural brown or pure white, and it is typically used for making envelopes or packaging.

Laminated paper Paper with a film applied to the surface for protection and to achieve a particular finish: either gloss or matt.

Linen paper Paper made with the fibres of the flax plant, which is one of the strongest and oldest vegetable fibres used by man.

Machine-made paper Modern type of paper that is produced on a continuous web using highly technological, computer controlled machinery.

Mould-made paper Paper made on a cylinder-mould machine, which closely resembles a handmade product. The making process is similar right up until the formation of the sheet, when the machine takes the place of the vatman, coucher and layer.

Mulberry paper This handmade paper from Korea, also known as hanji, is made from the inner bark of the Paper Mulberry plant. It is traditionally used in Korea to make a wide range of products from kites and fans to doors and floors.

Murano paper A naturally textured fine art paper, this has a 45% cotton content and comes in a variety colours. It is a versatile paper suitable for a broad range of projects.

Onion skin paper As its name suggests, this paper is thin and lightweight yet strong, and often translucent in appearance. It is durable and flexible, making it good for folding, due to its high cotton content.

Origami paper Lightweight paper is used for origami, to make folding easier. Origami paper is usually sold in prepackaged squares and commonly coloured on one side and white on the other.

Parchment paper Typically used for food preparation, this cellulose-based paper can be an interesting material to try in your projects, as it resists moisture and has translucent qualities. It is usually brown in colour.

Printing paper Also known as copier paper, this paper is universally used for photocopying and laser printing at home and in the office. It typically weighs between 70–90 gsm, and is arguably the most easily accessible paper for most people.

Sasawashi A fabric originating in Japan, made by cutting paper into a long, narrow strips, which are then twined, threaded and woven together.

Sugar paper The tough, coarse qualities of this paper made it useful for packaging bags of sugar, which is how it got its name. Also known as 'construction' paper, this is a versatile, general use material available in a wide range of colours and sheet sizes.

Tyvek A durable sheet made from polyethylene fibres, Tyvek is cuttable, but not tearable, and has many of the physical characteristics of paper.

Vellum Mammal skin prepared by cleaning, bleaching and stretching to make a surface smooth enough for writing and printing. Still used today for its durability to record Acts of Parliament.

Vellum paper A vegetable paper that imitates true vellum (made from mammal skin), but is instead made from plasticized cotton or wood fibres. It is popular for its semi-translucent appearance, and is heavier than standard tracing paper.

Washi This is the collective name for all handmade Japanese papers. It is commonly made using fibers from the bark of the Gampi tree.

Waxed paper Traditionally used in food preparation, this paper is made moisture-proof by the application of a thin layer of wax to its surface. Interesting cracking effects can be made by folding or crumpling this material, and it is useful in projects that are required to resist moisture.

glossary

Accordion fold A fold made of parallel pleats, which resembles the bellows of an accordion.

Adobe Illustrator Graphic design software used to create and edit illustrations.

Awl Pointed instrument used for piercing small holes in paper, wood and leather.

Barrel polisher Barrel-shaped machine used to polish the surface of metal.

Bench peg Support used in jewellery making that is made of wood and secured to a jeweller's work bench.

Bezel The metal rim in which a stone or object is set.

Bezel mandrel Jeweller's tool made of hardened steel and used to form bezel shapes.

Bezel pusher Polished steel tool used to push a bezel around the perimeter of a stone or object in jewellery making during setting.

Bézier Type of curve frequently used in computer-generated graphics.

Bitmap Digital image that is held in a computer's memory as a series of coloured dots in a grid.

Bookbinder's thread A 'no stretch' thread, strong enough to withstand the movement of a book and often waxed, which helps secure knots and improves strength and durability.

Brass brush Brush with brass bristles used to achieve a satin-effect 'brushed metal' finish on metal surfaces.

Burnishing Process in jewellery making where a smooth, hard tool is rubbed on the metal edge or surface to give a polished finish.

Cabochon Convex cut for a gemstone where the upper surface is gently domed and the base is flat; most often seen in an oval or circular shape.

Cellulose Main part of the cell wall in plants that may be broken down by beating and used to make paper.

Cleaning pickle Acid solution used by jewellers that removes the black oxide layer on metal surfaces formed during heating and soldering.

Collage The art of making pictures by sticking pieces of paper and other materials to a surface using glue.

Cold enamel Type of resin that is fused to the surface of metals, without the need for a kiln to create a decorative effect; available in a wide range of colours.

Collate In bookbinding, the process of gathering sections of paper or printed work in the correct sequence in preparation for binding.

Coptic binding Type of binding characterised by one or more sections of paper sewn through their folds and attached to each other with stitches across the spine.

CorelDraw Graphic design software used to create and edit illustrations.

Cotton linters Short fibres from around the cotton seed which are not suitable for spinning into thread for weaving.

Couch The action of transferring a wet sheet of paper pulp from a mould onto damp felt.

Creasing Linear indentation on paper made by hand or machine, which provides a hinge.

Cupboard fold Made by folding a square of paper in half, unfolding and folding the outside edges into the centre line.

Darning needle Long, large-eyed needle used for stitching thread; useful in various finishing processes, such as crochet.

Decoupage Decorative technique of covering a surface with cut-out shapes of paper.

Deckle Removable wooden frame that fits over a mould to contain pulp during the paper-making process.

Die cutting The process by which shapes are cut from paper or card with a metal die.

Engrave In laser cutting, to cut and score a design into paper using a laser beam.

EPS (Encapsulated PostScript) Digital file format for graphics.

Felt Woven blanket onto which sheets of newly-formed paper are turned out before pressing.

Fibre A long, narrow plant cell composed of cellulose, used as the basic element in paper making.

Findings Collective name for commercially-made jewellery fittings such as clasps and catches.

Fire brick Fire-resistant material used by jewellers as a soldering surface.

Fixative A liquid, similar to varnish, that is sprayed onto paper to preserve the surface and improve durability.

Flat file Tool used to clean and smooth surfaces of metal, especially after soldering.

Flux Chemical used in jewellery making to prevent oxidisation occurring on the surface of metals during soldering.

Format A particular way that information is encoded for storage in a computer file.

Fourdrinier machine The first papermaking machine to make continuous paper. Prior to its invention at the start of the 19th century, paper was made in single, separate sheets.

Fusing To blend two or more materials together by or as if by melting.

Gauge Standard of measurement such as the thickness of paper yarn.

Grain In paper, the alignment of fibres in industrial or mould-made paper.

Grammage Measurement of the grams per square meter, used to define stock paper weights.

GSM (Grams per square meter) Unit used to define stock paper weights.

Half round pliers Pliers where the cross section of the jaw end has one side half-round and the other side flat, often used to bend rings.

Hem An edge or border on a piece of material, stitched to finish an edge.

Hemp A tough, coarse fiber of the cannabis plant which can be used in paper making.

Herringbone Pattern of columns of short parallel lines with all the lines in one column sloping one way and lines in adjacent columns sloping the other.

Hide mallet Tool used for shaping and flattening metal, which does not leave marks on its surface.

Inkscape Graphic design software used to create and edit illustrations.

Invert To put in the opposite position, order or arrangement.

Kirigami Variation of origami that includes cutting the paper.

Kerf width The width of the slot made by a laser as it cuts.

Kettle stitch A bookbinding technique where a knot is tied in the thread that links one section of pages to the next.

Lacquer Clear or coloured coating used to give a durable, high-gloss finish to a surface.

Latex The milky sap of several trees that coagulates on exposure to air; used to make rubber.

Laser cutting A technology using a high-power laser, which is directed by a computer, to cut material.

Laser bed The surface on a laser-cutting machine where the material to be cut is positioned.

Lignin Substance found mainly in woody plants that rejects water and resists bonding, and must therefore be removed from the fibres before the papermaking process begins.

Machine laminating A specialised technique whereby paper is laminated by placing it between layers of plastic with heat and/or pressure, usually with an adhesive.

Matting pad Mildly abrasive pad used to achieve a satin-effect finish on the surface of metal.

Melchior Alloy of copper with nickel and sometimes zinc.

Mono-print A non-editionable print.

Mountain fold Fold used in origami where the crease will look like a raised ridge when unfolded.

Mould In paper making, the basic tool of a hand papermaker, consisting of a flat frame to which is fixed a mesh of brass wires or a woven cloth.

Nesting software Software useful in laser cutting, that was developed to enhance the efficiency and profitability for a sheet of material when designing using new technologies.

Node A connecting point where several lines come together in computer graphics.

Onyx Precious stone that occurs with a formation of straight and parallel bands of different colors, often black and white.

Open source Software that can be used, redistributed or rewritten, free of charge.

Papier mâché A 'mouldable' construction material made from paper mixed with wet paste, that solidifies when dry.

Paraffin Colourless wax that can be used as a coating for paper.

Piercing saw Jeweller's fine-bladed saw, used for cutting metal.

Pigment Substance used as a colouring.

Ply Single layer of paper or board.

PNG (Portable Network Graphic) Bitmapped file format used to hold image information.

Prototype An original, and usually working, model of a new product, or a new version of an existing product, made to check quality, proportions and accuracy.

Pulp The main ingredient in the paper-making process, usually made from processed wood, cotton linters or rags.

Pumice mild abrasive in light powder form, used as a polish in jewellery making.

Punching cradle Supporting surface for punching in signatures during book binding.

PVA glue White, water-based glue that becomes colourless when it dries appropriate for most book binding and paper projects.

Raster In laser cutting, a method used for engraving bitmap images, text and filled-in areas of a vector drawing file.

Repurpose To adapt for a different purpose.

Resin A compound that, when treated with a hardener, transforms from a viscous state to a solid material, which can be used as a sealant or cast into any shape.

RGBA In digital design, stands for red, green, blue, alpha. The values for red, green and blue specify the intensity of the colour in a given colour space, and the value for alpha determines the opacity of a given colour space.

Rivet To pass a metal pin or tube through two or more holes to hold two or more pieces of material together.

Plasti Dip An air-dried flexible liquid coating, which can be used in most paper projects as a moisture-resistant sealant.

Score An impression made into a sheet of paper or card to make folding easier and reduce the risk of the paper or card cracking.

Shibuichi An alloy of copper and silver extensively used in Japanese decorative art.

Shifu Japanese technique where Washi paper is cut into thin strips and twisted and woven to make cloth.

Size Water resistant starch or gelatin solution that is added to paper to decrease the paper's absorbency.

Solder Alloy with a low melting point used to fuse joins in metal.

Soldering torch Torch filled with gas that is used to provide heat during the soldering process.

SVG (Scalable Vector Graphics) Type of file format used to hold digital information about images or text.

Synthetic An artificial or manmade material.

Taper To make gradually smaller toward one end.

Tesselating To fit together exactly, leaving no space or gaps.

Thermal-kiss cutting A melting technique using a thermal die used by designers to create products with complex designs and intricate details, that would be otherwise unachievable with conventional steel-rule cutting dies.

Tin snips Shears designed to cut through thin sheets of metal.

Tool bar A row or column of selectable buttons in a computer program that allows the user to select from a variety of functions.

Upcycling Adding value through design to old or waste materials, often to create new products.

Valley fold Fold in origami where the crease drops downward, appearing like a valley between two hills.

Varnish A transparent, hard coating used to give protection and durability to a surface.

Vector graphics Digital images made from many individual objects (that are constructed from points connected by lines or nodes), with each of these objects having an individual property assigned to it, such as colour, fill or outline. This type of graphic can be scaled (enlarged or reduced) without any loss of quality.

Wet folding Origami technique that involves dampening the paper before folding, allowing for easier manipulation when forming curves and complex shapes.

Wire wool A bundle of strands of fine, soft steel filaments, used for finishing and polishing metal.

Yarn A continuous length of interlocking fibres used in textiles.

recommended suppliers

PAPER

G. F. Smith
www.gfsmith.com
+44 (0) 1482 323 503

Atlantis Art
www.atlantisart.co.uk
+44 (0) 20 7377 8855

Paperchase
www.paperchase.co.uk

John Purcell
www.johnpurcell.net
+44 (0) 207 737 5199

The Japanese Paper Place
www.japanesepaperplace.com
+1 (0) 416 538 9669

Arjo Wiggins
www.paperpoint.com
+44 (0) 1256 728 900

PAPER YARN

Paperphine
www.paperphine.com

Somic Textiles
www.somic.co.uk
+44 (0) 1772 790 000

Fibre Crafts
www.georgeweil.com
+44 (0) 1483 565 800

Hand Weavers Studio and Gallery
www.handweavers.co.uk
+44 (0) 20 7272 1891

Habu Textiles
www.habutextiles.com
+1 (0) 212 239 3546

Taito Pirkanmaa
www.taitopirkanmaa.fi
+358 (0) 3 2251 400

HOOK AND DARNING NEEDLE

Yarnsmith
www.yarnsmith.co.uk
+44 (0) 1787 881 620

Purplelinda Crafts
www.purplelindacrafts.co.uk

Fibre Crafts
www.georgeweil.com
+44 (0) 1483 565 800

Or try your local haberdashery, or the haberdashery section in your nearest department store.

BOOKBINDING TOOLS AND MATERIALS

Shepherds
www.bookbinding.co.uk
+44 (0) 20 7233 5298

J. Hewit and Sons Ltd
www.hewit.com
+44 (0) 1506 444 160

Ratchford Ltd
www.ratchford.co.uk
+44 (0) 161 480 8484

Hollanders
www.hollanders.com
+1 (0) 734 741 7531

SILVERSMITHING TOOLS AND MATERIALS

Cooksons
www.cooksongold.com
+44 (0) 845 100 1122

Rashbel
www.rashbel.com
+ 44 (0) 20 7831 5646

HS Walsh and Sons Ltd
www.hswalsh.com
+44 (0) 1959 543 660

Kernowcraft
www.kernowcraft.com
+ 44 (0) 1872 573 888

Betts metals
www.bettsmetals.com
+ 44 (0) 121 233 2413

PAPER MAKING MATERIALS

Paper Shed
www.georgeweil.com
+44 (0) 1483 565 800

Falkiners fine papers
www.falkiners.com
+44 (0) 20 7831 1151

Twinrocker handmade paper
www.twinrocker.com
+1 (0) 800 757 8946

Talas
www.talasonline.com
+1 (0) 212 219 0770

LASER CUTTING

Razor lab
www.razorlab.co.uk
+44 (0) 20 7831 3301

Inscribe Ltd
www.laz3r.com
+44 (0) 1509 550 203

Cut Laser Cut
www.cutlasercut.com
+ 44 (0) 20 3490 9886

Zap Creatives
www.zapcreatives.co.uk

FOR LASER RESEARCH, INNOVATION AND PRODUCT DEVELOPMENT

Jewellery Industry Innovation Centre
www.jewellery-innovation.co.uk
+ 44 (0) 121 331 5940

Metropolitan Works
www.metropolitanworks.org
+ 44 (0) 20 7320 1878

Ponoko
www.ponoko.com

RIBBONS

The Ribbon Shop
www.theribbonshop.co.uk
+ 44 (0) 020 8974 5074

MacCulloch and Wallis
www.macculloch-wallis.co.uk
+ 44 (0) 20 7629 0311

RESINS

Canonbury Arts
www.canonburyarts.co.uk
+ 44 (0) 20 7226 4652

C. J. Resins
www.cjresins.co.uk
+ 44 (0) 1242 602 739

COLOURANTS AND DYES

Specialist Crafts
www.specialistcrafts.co.uk
+ 44 (0) 116 269 7711

John Lewis
www.johnlewis.com
+ 44 (0) 8456 049 049

recommended reading

CHAPTER 1

Adams, Maia, *Fashion Jewellery: Catwalk and Couture* (London: Laurence King Publishing Ltd, 2010)

Akabane, Natsumi (ed), *Encyclopaedia of Paper-Folding Designs* (Tokyo: PIE books, 2001)

Avella, Natalie, *Paper Engineering: 3-D Design Techniques for a 2-D Material* (Hove: Rotovision, 2006)

Ramshaw, Wendy and Watkins, David, *The Paper Jewellery Collection: Pop-out Artwear* (London: Thames & Hudson, 2000)

Schmidt, Petra and Stattmann, Nicola, *Unfolded: Paper in Design, Art, Architecture and Industry*, (3rd edn) (Basle: Birkhauser Verlag AG, 2009)

Yoshida, Miyuki, *Paper Folding for Pop-up* (Tokyo: PIE books, 2008)

Zidianakis, Vassilis (ed.), *RRRIIPP! Paper Fashion* (Athens: ATOPOS Contemporary Visual Culture, 2007)

CHAPTER 2

Donath, Uta, Hauck, Eva and , Hoffmann Petra, *Paper Yarn: 24 Creative Projects to Make Using a Variety of Techniques* (New York: St Martin's Press, 2009)

Eaton, Jan, *Compendium of Crochet Techniques* (Tunbridge Wells: Search Press Ltd, 2008)

Harding, Sally, *Quick Crochet Huge Hooks* (London: Mitchell Beazley, 2005)

Leitner, Christina, *Paper Textiles* (London: A&C Black Publishers, 2005)

McEneely, Naomi, *Interweave's Compendium of Finishing Techniques: Crochet, Embroidery, Knitting, Knotting, Weaving* (Colorado: Interweave Press Inc, 2003)

Stoller, Debbie, *Stitch 'n Bitch Crochet: The Happy Hooker* (New York: Workman Publishing, 2006)

Taimina, Daina, *Crochet Adventures with Hyperbolic Planes* (Wellesley: A K Peters/CRC Press, 2009)

CHAPTER 3

Abbott, Kathy, *Bookbinding: A Step-by-step Guide* (Ramsbury: Crowood Press Ltd, 2010)

Doggett, Sue, *Handmade Books* (London: A & C Black Publishers Ltd, 2003)

Doggett, Sue, *The Bookbinding Handbook: Simple Techniques and Step-by-Step Projects* (Tunbridge Wells: Search Books, 2008)

Stein, Jeannine, *Re-bound: Creating Handmade Books from Recycled and Repurposed Materials* (Beverly, Mass: Quarry Books, 2009)

Thompson, Jason, *Playing with Books: Upcycling, Deconstructing and Reimagining the Book* (Beverly, Mass: Quarry Books, 2010)

Weston, Heather, *Bookcraft: Techniques for Binding, Folding, and Decorating to Create Books and More* (Massachusetts: Quarry Books, 2008)

CHAPTER 4

Bradley, Alexandra and Fernandes, Gavin (ed.), *Unclasped: Contemporary British Jewellery* (London: Black Dog Publishing, 2001)

Falk, Fritz and Chadour-Sampson, Beatriz, *David Watkins: Artist in Jewellery* (Stuttgart: Arnoldsche, 2008)

Haywood, Joanne, Mixed-media Jewellery: *Methods and Techniques (*A & C Black Publishers Ltd, 2009)

Mansell, Amanda, *Adorn: New Jewellery* (London: Laurence King, 2008)

Olver, Liz, *The Art of Jewellery Design* (London: A & C Black Publishers Ltd, 2002)

Seecherran, Vannetta, *Contemporary Jewellery Making Techniques: A Comprehensive Guide for Jewellers and Metalsmiths* (Tunbridge Wells: Search Press Ltd, 2009)

CHAPTER 5

Dorit, Elisha, *Printmaking and Mixed Media: Simple Techniques and Projects for Paper and Fabric* (Colorado: Interweave Press Inc, 2009)

Holmes, Cas, *The Found Object in Textile Art* (London: Batsford, 2010)

Plowman, John, *Papermaking Techniques Book: Over 50 Techniques for Making and Embellishing Handmade Paper* (Hove: Apple Press, 2001)

Reimer-Epp, Heidi and Reimer, Mary, *The Encyclopedia of Papermaking and Bookbinding: The Definitive Guide to Making, Embellishing and Repairing Paper and Books* (London: British Library, 2002)

Thomas, Jane and Jackson, Paul, *On Paper: New Paper Art* (London: Merrell Holberton, 2001)

Turner, Silvie, *The Book of Fine Paper* (London: Thames and Hudson, 1998)

CHAPTER 6

Heyenga, Laura, Ryan, Rob, and Avella, Natalie, *Paper Cutting* (San Francisco: Chronicle Books, 2011)

Klanten, Robert, Ehmann, S., Meyer, B., *Papercraft: Design and Art with Paper,* (Berlin: Die Gestalten Verlag, 2009)

Revere McFadden, David, *Slash: Paper Under the Knife* (Milan: 5 Continents Editions, 2009)

Sloman, Paul (ed.), *Paper: Tear, Fold, Rip, Crease, Cut* (London: Black Dog Publishing, 2009)

van Berkum, Ans, *Nel Linssen Papieren Sieraden (Paper Jewellery)* (Nijmegen: N. Linssen, 2002)

van Sicklen, Margaret, *Modern Paper Crafts: A 21st-Century Guide to Folding, Cutting, Scoring, Pleating, and Recycling* (New York: Stewart, Tabori & Chang Inc, 2011)

bibliography

Adams, Maia, *Fashion Jewellery: Catwalk and Couture* (London: Laurence King Publishing Ltd, 2010)

Akabane, Natsumi, *Encyclopaedia of Paper-Folding Designs* (Tokyo: PIE books, 2001)

Bradley, Alexandra and Fernandes, Gavin (ed.), *Unclasped: Contemporary British Jewellery* (London: Black Dog Publishing, 1997)

van Berkum, Ans, *Nel Linssen Papieren Sieraden (Paper Jewellery)* (Nijmegen: N. Linssen, 2002)

Leitner, Christina, *Paper Textiles* (London: A&C Black Publishers Ltd, 2005)

Ramshaw, Wendy and Watkins, David, *The Paper Jewellery Collection: Pop-out Artwear* (London: Thames & Hudson, 2000)

Revere McFadden, David, *Slash: Paper Under the Knife* (Milan: 5 Continents Editions, 2009)

Falk, Fritz and Chadour-Sampson, Beatriz, *David Watkins: Artist in Jewellery* (Stuttgart: Arnoldsche, 2008)

Zidianakis, Vassilis (ed.), *RRRIIPP! Paper Fashion* (Athens: ATOPOS Contemporary Visual Culture, 2007)

Doggett, Sue, *The Bookbinding Handbook: Simple Techniques and Step-by-Step Projects* (Tunbridge Wells: Search Books, 2008)

Sloman, Paul (ed.), *Paper: Tear, Fold, Rip, Crease, Cut* (London: Black Dog Publishing, 2009)

Weston, Heather, *Bookcraft: Techniques for Binding, Folding, and Decorating to Create Books and More* (Minneapolis: Quarry Books, 2008)

Thomas, Jane and Jackson, Paul, *On Paper: New Paper Art* (London: Merrell Holberton, 2001)

index